The Non-Designer's Design Book

THIRD EDITION

design
and
typographic
principles
for the
visual
novice

Robin Williams

Peachpit Press
Berkeley
California

The Non-Designer's Design Book
third edition
ROBIN WILLIAMS

©2008 by Robin Williams

Peachpit Press
1249 Eighth Street
Berkeley, California 94710
510.524.2178
510.524.2221 FAX

Editor:	Nancy Davis
Interior design:	Robin Williams
Production:	Robin Williams
Cover design and production:	John Tollett

Peachpit Press is a division of Pearson Education.

Find us on the web at www.Peachpit.com.

To report errors, please send a note to errata@peachpit.com.

The quote by Jan White on page 187 is from the out-of-print book *How to Spec Type*, by Alex White. Reprinted courtesy of Roundtable Press, Inc. Copyright 1987 by Roundtable Press, Inc.

The portions of "Ladle Rat Rotten Hut" and other stories, such as "Guilty Looks Enter Tree Beers," "Center Alley," and "Violate Huskings" are from a long out-of-print book by Howard L. Chace called *Anguish Languish.* It is our understanding that these delightful stories are now in the public domain. They are easily found on the Internet.

ISBN 13: 978-0-321-53404-0

ISBN 10: 0-321-53404-2

10 9 8 7

Printed and bound in the United States of America

*M*ore matter is being printed and published today than ever before, and every publisher of an advertisement, pamphlet, or book expects his material to be read. Publishers and, even more so, readers want what is important to be clearly laid out. They will not read anything that is troublesome to read, but are pleased with what looks clear and well arranged, for it will make their task of understanding easier. For this reason, the important part must stand out and the unimportant must be subdued . . . .

The technique of modern typography must also adapt itself to the speed of our times. Today, we cannot spend as much time on a letter heading or other piece of jobbing as was possible even in the nineties.

Jan Tschichold 1935

The **function** of Readability is often ta-ken too literally and over-emphasized at the Cost of INDIVIDUALITY.

Paul Rand 1914 · 1996

typefaces

Miss Fajardose

Garamond Premier Pro Regular *and Italic*

Type Embellishments One

typefaces

flyswim

Schablone Rough

Helvetica Regular

Schablone Labelrough Positive

Contents

Design Principles

Designing With Type

Extras

It stinks.

Herb Lubalin

But, is it appropriate?
Edward Gottschall

Is this book for you?

This book is written for all the people who need to design pages, but have no background or formal training in design. I don't mean just those who are designing fancy packaging or lengthy brochures—I mean the assistants whose bosses now tell them to design the newsletters, church volunteers who are providing information to their congregations, small business owners who are creating their own advertising, students who understand that a better-looking paper often means a better grade, professionals who realize that an attractive presentation garners greater respect, teachers who have learned that students respond more positively to information that is well laid out, statisticians who see that numbers and stats can be arranged in a way that invites reading rather than sleeping, and on and on.

This book assumes you don't have the time or interest to study design and typography, but would like to know how to make your pages look better. Well, the premise of this book is age-old: knowledge is power. Most people can look at a poorly designed page and state that they don't like it, but they don't know what to do to fix it. In this book I will point out four basic concepts that are used in virtually every well-designed job. These concepts are clear and concrete. If you don't know what's wrong with it, how can you fix it? Once you recognize the concepts, you will notice whether or not they have been applied to your pages. *Once you can name the problem, you can find the solution.*

This book is not intended to take the place of four years of design school. I do not pretend you will automatically become a brilliant designer after you read this little book. But I do guarantee you will never again look at a page in the same way. I guarantee if you follow these basic principles, your work will look more professional, organized, unified, and interesting. And you will feel empowered.

With a smile, *Robin*

The Joshua Tree Epiphany

This short chapter explains the **four basic principles** in general, each of which will be explained in detail in the following chapters. But first I want to tell you a little story that made me realize the importance of being able to name things, since *naming* these principles is the key to having power over them.

Many years ago I received a tree identification book for Christmas. I was at my parents' home, and after all the gifts had been opened I decided to go out and identify the trees in the neighborhood. Before I went out, I read through part of the book. The first tree in the book was the Joshua tree because it only took two clues to identify it. Now, the Joshua tree is a really weird-looking tree and I looked at that picture and said to myself, "Oh, we don't have that kind of tree in Northern California. That is a weird-looking tree. I would know if I saw that tree, and I've never seen one before."

So I took my book and went outside. My parents lived in a cul-de-sac of six homes. Four of those homes had Joshua trees in the front yards. I had lived in that house for thirteen years, and I had never seen a Joshua tree. I took a walk around the block, and there must have been a sale at the nursery when everyone was landscaping their new homes—at least 80 percent of the homes had Joshua trees in the front yards. *And I had never seen one before!* Once I was conscious of the tree—once I could name it—I saw it everywhere. Which is exactly my point: Once you can name something, you're conscious of it. You have power over it. You own it. You're in control.

So now you're going to learn the names of several design principles. And you are going to be in control of your pages.

Good Design Is As Easy as 1-2-3

1. Learn the principles.
They're simpler than you might think.
2. Recognize when you're not using them.
Put it into words -- name the problem.
3. Apply the principles.
You'll be amazed.

typefaces
Times New Roman Regular
and Bold

Good design
is as easy as . . .

1 **Learn the principles.**
They're simpler than you might think.

2 **Recognize when you're not using them.**
Put it into words — name the problem.

3 **Apply the principles.**
You'll be amazed.

typefaces
Univers 75 Black
Univers 65 Bold
Cochin Italic
Potrzebie (numbers)

The four basic principles

The following is a brief overview of the basic principles of design that appear in every well-designed piece of work. Although I discuss each one of these principles separately, keep in mind they are really interconnected. Rarely will you apply only one principle.

Contrast

The idea behind contrast is to avoid elements on the page that are merely *similar.* If the elements (type, color, size, line thickness, shape, space, etc.) are not the *same,* then make them **very different.** Contrast is often the most important visual attraction on a page—it's what makes a reader look at the page in the first place.

Repetition

Repeat visual elements of the design throughout the piece. You can repeat colors, shapes, textures, spatial relation-ships, line thicknesses, fonts, sizes, graphic concepts, etc. This develops the organization and strengthens the unity.

Alignment

Nothing should be placed on the page arbitrarily. Every element should have some visual connection with another element on the page. This creates a clean, sophisticated, fresh look.

Proximity

Items relating to each other should be grouped close together. When several items are in close proximity to each other, they become one visual unit rather than several separate units. This helps organize information, reduces clutter, and gives the reader a clear structure.

Umm . . .

When gathering these four principles from the vast maze of design theory, I thought there must be some appropriate and memorable acronym within these conceptual ideas that would help people remember them. Well, uh, there is a memorable—but rather inappropriate—acronym. Sorry.

Good
communication
is as

stimulating

as black coffee . . .

and just
as hard
to sleep after.

ANNE MORROW LINDBERGH

typefaces
Mona Lisa Solid
Escalido Gothico

Proximity

Very often in the work of new designers, the words and phrases and graphics are strung out all over the place, filling corners and taking up lots of room so there won't be any empty space. There seems to be a fear of empty space. When pieces of a design are scattered all over, the page appears unorganized and the information may not be instantly accessible to the reader.

Robin's Principle of Proximity states that you **group related items together,** move them physically close to each other so the related items are seen as one cohesive group rather than a bunch of unrelated bits.

Items or groups of information that are *not* related to each other should *not* be in close proximity (nearness) to the other elements, which gives the reader an instant visual clue to the organization and content of the page.

A very simple example illustrates this concept. In the list below, on the left side, what do you assume about all those flowers? Probably that they have something in common, right? In the list below-right, what do you assume? It appears that the last four flowers are somehow different from the others. You understand this *instantly.* And you understand it without even being conscious of it. You *know* the last four flowers are somehow different *because they are physically separated from the rest of the list.* That's the concept of proximity—on a page (as in life), **physical closeness implies a relationship.**

My Flowers

Marigold
Pansy
Rue
Woodbine
Daisy
Cowslip
Carnation
Primrose
Violets
Pink

My Flowers

Marigold
Pansy
Rue
Woodbine
Daisy
Cowslip

Carnation
Primrose
Violets
Pink

typefaces
Spring Regular
Formata Light

Take a look at this typical business card layout, below. How many separate elements do you see in that small space? That is, how many times does your eye stop to look at something?

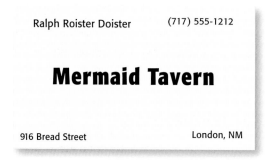

Does your eye stop five times? Of course—there are five separate items on this little card.

Where do you begin reading? In the middle, probably, because that phrase is boldest.

What do you read next—left to right (because it's in English)?

What happens when you get to the bottom-right corner, where does your eye go?

Do you wander around making sure you didn't miss any corners?

And what if I confuse the issue even further:

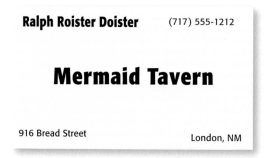

Now that there are two bold phrases, where do you begin? Do you start in the upper left? Do you start in the center?

After you read those two items, where do you go? Perhaps you bounce back and forth between the words in bold, nervously trying to also catch the words in the corners.

Do you know when you're finished?

Does your friend follow the same pattern you did?

When several items are in close proximity to each other, they become *one* visual unit rather than several *separate* units. As in life, **the proximity, or the closeness, implies a relationship.**

By grouping similar elements into one unit, several things instantly happen: The page becomes more organized. You understand where to begin reading the message, and you know when you are finished. And the "white space" (the space around the letters) automatically becomes more organized as well.

A problem with the previous card is that not one of the items on the card seems related to any other item. It is not clear where you should begin reading the card, and it is not clear when you are finished.

If I do one thing to this business card—**if I group related elements together, into closer proximity**—see what happens:

Mermaid Tavern
Ralph Roister Doister

916 Bread Street
London, NM
(717) 555-1212

Now is there any question about where you begin to read the card? Where do your eyes go next? Do you know when you're finished?

With that one simple concept, this card is now organized both **intellectually** and **visually.** And thus it communicates more clearly.

typefaces
Formata Light
Formata Bold Condensed

Shown below is a typical newsletter flag (sometimes called masthead). How many separate elements are in this piece? Does any item of information seem related to any other, judging from the placement?

Take a moment to decide which items should be grouped into closer proximity and which should be separated.

typefaces
Palatino Light
and Italic
Wade Sans Light

The two items on the top left are in close proximity to each other, implying a relationship. But **should** these two have a relationship? Is it the Society that's amusing and peculiar, or "The Shakespeare Papers"?

How about the volume number and date? They should be close together since they both identify this particular issue.

In the example below, the proper relationships have been established.

Notice I did a couple of other things along the way:

I changed everything from all caps to lowercase with appropriate capitals, which gave me room to make the title bigger and stronger.

I changed the corners from rounded to straight, giving the piece a cleaner, stronger look.

I enlarged the swan and overlapped the edge with it. Don't be a wimp.

Because the text is going to drop out of the dark background, I changed the small font to Trebuchet so it wouldn't fall apart when printed.

When you create a flyer, a brochure, a newsletter, or whatever, you already know which pieces of information are logically connected, you *know* which information should be emphasized and what can be de-emphasized. Express that information graphically by grouping it.

Correspondences
Flowers, herbs, trees, weeds
Ancient Greeks and Romans
Historical characters
Quotes on motifs
Women
Death
Morning
Snakes
Language
Iambic pentameter
Rhetorical devices
Poetic devices
First lines
Collections
Small printings
Kitschy
Dingbats
Thematic
Villains and saints
Drinks and recipes
Music
Quizzes
Fun but difficult quizzes

Correspondences
Flowers, herbs, trees, weeds
Ancient Greeks and Romans
Historical characters

Quotes on motifs
Women
Death
Morning
Snakes

Language
Iambic pentameter
Rhetorical devices
Poetic devices
First lines

Collections
Small printings
Kitschy
Dingbats

Thematic
Villains and saints
Drinks and recipes
Music

Quizzes
Fun but difficult quizzes

typefaces
Warnock Pro Light
and Bold
Formata Bold

Obviously, this list needs some formatting to make it understandable. But the biggest problem with this list is that everything is close to everything else, so there is no way to see the relationships or the organization.

The same list has been visually separated into groups. I'm sure you already do this automatically—I'm just suggesting that you now do it **consciously** and thus with more strength.

Notice I added some **contrast** to the headlines and **repeated** that contrast.

Sometimes when grouping items into close proximity, you need to make some changes, such as in the size or weight or placement of text or graphics. Body copy (the main bulk of reading text) does not have to be 12 point! Information that is subsidiary to the main message, such as the volume number and year of a newsletter, can often be as small as 7 or 8 point.

First Friday Club
Winter Reading Schedule

Friday November 1 at 5 p.m. *Cymbeline*
In this action-packed drama, our strong and true heroine, Imogen, dresses as a boy and runs off to a cave in Wales to avoid marrying a man she hates.
Friday, December 6, 5 p.m. *The Winter's Tale*
The glorious Paulina and the steadfast Hermione keep a secret together for sixteen years, until the Delphic Oracle is proven true and the long-lost daughter is found.
All readings held at the Mermaid Tavern, Grand Hall. Sponsored by the Community Education Program. Tickets $10 and $8
For ticket information phone 555-1212
Also Friday, January 3 at 5 p.m. *Twelfth Night*
Join us as Olivia survives a shipwreck, dresses as a man, gets a job, and finds both a man and a woman in love with her.

typefaces
Anna Nicole
Formata Regular

Not only is this page visually boring (nothing pulls your eyes in to the body copy to take a look), but it is difficult to find the information—exactly what is going on, where is it happening, what time is it at, etc. It doesn't help that the information is presented inconsistently.

For instance, how many readings are in the series?

The idea of proximity doesn't mean that *everything* is closer together; it means elements that are *intellectually connected,* those that have some sort of communication relationship, should also be *visually connected.* Other separate elements or groups of elements should *not* be in close proximity. The closeness *or* lack of closeness indicates the relationship.

First Friday Club
Winter Reading Schedule

Cymbeline
In this action-packed drama, our strong and true heroine, Imogen, dresses as a boy and runs off to a cave in Wales to avoid marrying a man she hates.
November 1 • Friday • 5 P.M.

The Winter's Tale
The glorious Paulina and the steadfast Hermione keep a secret together for sixteen years, until the Delphic Oracle is proven true and the long-lost daughter found.
December 6 • Friday • 5 P.M.

Twelfth Night
Join us as Olivia survives a shipwreck, dresses as a man, gets a job, and finds both a man and a woman in love with her.
January 6 • Friday • 5 P.M.

The Mermaid Tavern
All readings are held at The Mermaid Tavern in the Grand Hall
Sponsored by the Community Education Program
Tickets $10 and $8
For ticket information phone 555.1212

typefaces
Anna Nicole
Formata Regular
and Light Condensed

How many readings are in the series?

First I intellectually grouped the information together (in my head or sketched onto paper), then physically set the text in groups on the page. Notice the spacing between the three readings is the same, indicating that these three groups are somehow related.

The subsidiary information is farther away—you **instantly** know it is not one of the readings, even if you can't see it clearly.

Below you see a similar example to the one on the previous page. Glance at it quickly—now what do you assume about the three readings?

And why exactly do you assume one reading is different from the others? Because one is separate from the others. You instantly know that event is somehow different *because of the spatial relationships.*

First Friday Club
Summer Reading Schedule

1 Henry IV
Still trying to get to the Holy Land to atone for Richard's death, Henry is beset by many troubles, including the willing debauchery of his son, Hal. Because these Henry plays are closely connected, we're going to read them both in one day.
June 4 • Friday • 1 P.M.

2 Henry IV
We carry on with the tales of Falstaff and Hal. Hal proves to his father he is a decent son and heartbreakingly rejects his good round friend Falstaff.
June 4 • Friday • 6 P.M.

Henry V
Does Hal really have to be so cruel to his friends? Is that what being a king is all about? Hal, now Henry V, marches into France to win Agincourt.
July 8 • Friday • 5 P.M.

The Mermaid Tavern
All readings are held at The Mermaid Tavern in the Grand Hall
Sponsored by the Community Education Program
Tickets $10 and $8, each play
For ticket information phone 555.1212

It's really amazing how much information we get from a quick glance at a page. Thus it becomes your responsibility to make sure the reader gets the **correct** information.

The designer's intention with this dance postcard was probably to create something fun and energetic, but at first glance, can you tell when and where the classes are happening?

By using the principle of proximity to organize the information (as shown below), we can communicate immediately who, what, when, and where. We don't run the risk of losing potential customers because they give up searching through the vast field of slanted text.

Don't feel like you have to somehow portray "dancing" (in this case) through your design. At this point, if your choice is between clear communication or amateur design, choose clear communication. Upgrading your design skills is a gradual process and **begins with clear communication.**

Learn to Dance!
Rosetta Dance Studio • 109 Jive Lane • Saturdays 9 a.m. to 3 p.m.

Smooth	Rhythm	Street	Social
Waltz	Cha Cha	Hip Hop	East Coast Swing
Tango	Rumba	Krump	West Coast Swing
Foxtrot	Bolero	Funk	Lindy Hop
Quickstep	Mambo	Clown	Salsa

With or without a partner!
Prizes! Free Tea and Scones!

typeface
Jiggery Pokery

You're probably already using the principle of proximity in your work, but you may not be pushing it as far as you could to make it truly effective. Really look at those pages, at those elements, and see which items *should* be grouped together.

Want to be an

UNDERSTANDER?

How'd you like to . . .

understand every word and every nuance in a Shakespeare play?

Can you imagine . . .

going to see a play performed and actually understanding everything that's going on?

What if you could. . .

laugh in the right places in a play, cry in the right places, boo and hiss in the right places?

Ever wanted to . . .

talk to someone about a Shakespearean play and have that person think you know what you're talking about?

Would you like to . . .

have people admire and even esteem you because you know whether or not Portia cheated her father by telling Bassanio which casket to choose?

It's all possible.

Live the life you've dreamed about!

Be an Understander!

For more info on how to wisen up and start your new life as an Understander, contact us right away: **phone: 1-800-555-1212;** email: **Ben@TheUnderstanders.com**

typefaces
Clarendon Bold
and Roman

The person who designed this mini-poster typed two Returns after each headline **and** paragraph. Thus the headlines are each the same distance from the body copy above and below, making the heads and body copy pieces appear as separate, unconnected items. You can't tell if the headline belongs to the text above it or below it because the distances are the same.

There is lots of white space available here, but it's all broken up. And there is white space where it doesn't belong, like between the headlines and their related texts. When white space is "trapped" like this, it tends to visually push the elements apart.

Group the items that have relationships. If there are areas on the page where the organization is not perfectly clear, see if items are in proximity that *shouldn't* be. Use the simple design feature of space to make the page not only more organized, but nicer to look at.

Want to be an
UNDERSTANDER?

How'd you like to . . .
understand every word and every
nuance in a Shakespeare play?

Can you imagine . . .
going to see a play performed and actually
understanding everything that's going on?

What if you could. . .
laugh in the right places in a play,
cry in the right places, boo and hiss
in the right places?

Ever wanted to . . .
talk to someone about a Shakespearean play
and have that person think you know what
you're talking about?

Would you like to . . .
have people admire and even esteem you
because you know whether or not Portia
cheated her father by telling Bassanio
which casket to choose?

It's all possible!
Live the life you've dreamed about—
be an Understander!

For more info on how to wisen up and start your
new life as an Understander, contact us right away:
   1.800.555.1212
   Ben@TheUnderstanders.com

typefaces
**Clarendon
Bold,** Roman,
and Light

If I do just one thing to this piece, if I move the headlines closer to their related paragraphs of text, several things happen:

   The organization is clearer.

   The white space is not trapped within elements.

   There appears to be more room on the page.

I also put the phone and email address on separate lines—but grouped together and separated—so they'll stand out as important information.

And you probably noticed that I changed the centered alignment to flush left (that's the principle of **alignment,** as explained in the next chapter), which created more room so I could enlarge the graphic.

Proximity is really just a matter of being a little more conscious, of doing what you do naturally, but pushing the concept a little further. Once you become aware of the importance of the relationships between lines of type, you will start noticing its effect. Once you start noticing the effect, you own it, you have power over it, you are in control.

Gertrude's Piano Bar

STARTERS:
GERTRUDE'S FAMOUS ONION LOAF - 8
GAZPACHO OR ASPARAGUS-SPINACH SOUP - 7
SUMMER GARDEN TOMATO SALAD - 8
SLICED VINE-RIPENED YELLOW AND RED
TOMATOES WITH FRESH MOZZARELLA AND BASIL
BALSAMIC VINAIGRETTE
HAMLET'S CHOPPED SALAD - 7
CUBED CUCUMBERS, RADISHES, AVOCADO,
TOMATOES, JARLSBERG CHEESE, AND ROMAINE
LEAVES TOSSED IN A LIGHT LEMON VINAIGRETTE
CAESAR SALAD - 7
HOUSE-MADE DRESSING, PARMESAN AND
CROUTONS
CARIBBEAN CEVICHE - 9
LIME-MARINATED BABY SCALLOPS WITH RED
PEPPER, ONIONS, CILANTRO, JALAPENOS, AND
ORANGE JUICE
SHRIMP COCKTAIL - 14
FIVE LARGE SHRIMP WITH HOUSE-MADE COCKTAIL
SAUCE
ENTREES:
NEW YORK STEAK, 16 OZ - 27
ROTISSERIE CHICKEN - 17
FRESH FISH, 10 OZ - MARKET PRICE
GRILLED SHRIMP - 24
NEW ORLEANS LUMP CRAB CAKES
WITH WARM VEGETABLE COLESLAW, MASHED
POTATOES, SPINACH AND ROMESCO SAUCE - 18
GRILLED PORTOBELLO MUSHROOM
STUFFED WITH RICOTTA CHEESE, GARLIC, ONIONS
AND SPINACH, SERVED OVER MASHED POTATOES
- 18
NEW ZEALAND RACK OF LAMB - 26
BARBEQUED BABY BACK RIBS - 24
AUSTRALIAN LOBSTER TAIL, 10 OZ - MARKET PRICE
SURF & TURF
AUSTRALIAN LOBSTER & 8OZ FILET - MARKET
PRICE

typefaces
Potrzebie
Times New Roman

Lest you think no menu could be this bad, know that I took it right out of a restaurant. Really. The biggest problem, of course, is that all the information is one big chunk.

Before trying to design with this information, write out the separate pieces of information that belong together; group the elements. You know how to do this—simply use your brain.

Once you have the groups of information, you can play with them on the page. You have a computer—try lots of options. Learn how to format a page in your software.

In the example below, I put *more* space between the separate menu items. Of course, one should almost never use all caps because they are so hard to read, so I changed it to caps and lowercase. And I made the type a couple of point sizes smaller, both of which gave me a lot more room to work with so I could put more space between the elements.

Gertrude's Piano Bar

Starters

Gertrude's Famous Onion Loaf - 8

Gazpacho or Asparagus-Spinach Soup - 7

Summer Garden Tomato Salad - 8
sliced vine-ripened yellow and red tomatoes
with fresh mozzarella and basil Balsamic vinaigrette

Hamlet's Chopped Salad - 7
cubed cucumbers, radishes, avocado, tomatoes, Jarlsberg
cheese, and romaine leaves tossed in a light lemon vinaigrette

Caesar Salad - 7
house-made dressing, Parmesan, and croutons

Caribbean Ceviche - 9
lime-marinated baby scallops with red pepper, onions, cilantro,
jalapenos, and orange juice

Shrimp Cocktail - 14
five large shrimp with house-made cocktail sauce

Entrees

New York steak, 16 ounce - 27

Rotisserie Chicken - 17

Fresh Fish, 10 ounce - Market Price

Grilled Shrimp - 24

New Orleans Lump Crab Cakes - 18
with warm vegetable coleslaw, mashed potatoes, spinach,
and Romesco sauce

Grilled Portobello Mushroom - 18
stuffed with Ricotta cheese, garlic, onions and spinach,
served over mashed potatoes

New Zealand Rack of Lamb - 26

Barbequed Baby Back Ribs - 24

Australian Lobster Tail, 10 ounce - Market Price

Surf & Turf
Australian Lobster & 8 ounce Filet - Market Price

typefaces
Potrzebie
Times New Roman Bold
and Regular

The biggest problem with the original menu is that there is no separation of information. In your software, learn how to format so you can make exactly the amount of space you need before and after each element.

The original text in all caps took up all the space so there was no extra, blank, "white" space to rest your eyes. The more text you have, the less you can get away with all caps. And it's okay to set the type smaller than 12 point! Really!

In the example on the previous page, we still have a little bit of a problem separating the "Starters" and the "Entrees." Let's indent each section—watch how the extra space defines these two groups even further, yet clearly communicates that they are still similar groups. (I enlarged the size of "Starters" and "Entrees" also, which is the principle of Contrast.)

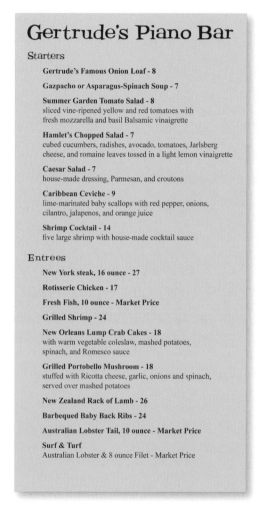

We really don't have enough room to add more space before "Starters" and "Entrees," but we do have room to make an indent. That extra space under the heading helps to separate these two groups of information. It's all about space.

Rarely is the principle of proximity the only answer to a page. The other three principles are intrinsic to the design process and you will usually find yourself using all four. But take them one at a time—start with proximity. In the example below, you can imagine how all of the other principles would mean nothing if I didn't first apply the appropriate spacing.

Gertrude's Piano Bar

Starters

Gertrude's Famous Onion Loaf	8
Gazpacho or Asparagus-Spinach Soup	7
Summer Garden Tomato Salad	8
sliced vine-ripened yellow and red tomatoes with fresh mozzarella and basil Balsamic vinaigrette	
Hamlet's Chopped Salad	7
cubed cucumbers, radishes, scallions, avocado, tomatoes, jarlsberg cheese, and romaine leaves tossed in a light lemon vinaigrette	
Caesar Salad	7
house-made dressing, Parmesan, and croutons	
Caribbean Ceviche	9
lime-marinated baby scallops with red pepper, onions, cilantro, jalapenos, and orange juice	
Shrimp Cocktail	14
five large shrimp with house-made cocktail sauce	

Entrees

New York Steak, 16 ounce	27
Rotisserie Chicken	17
Fresh Fish, 10 ounce	Market Price
Grilled Shrimp	24
New Orleans Lump Crab Cakes	18
with warm vegetable coleslaw, mashed potatoes, spinach, and Romesco sauce	
Grilled Portobello Mushroom	18
stuffed with ricotta cheese, garlic, onions and spinach, served over mashed potatoes	
New Zealand Rack of Lamb	26
Barbequed Baby Back Ribs	24
Australian Lobster Tail, 10 ounce	Market Price
Surf & Turf: Australian Rock Lobster & 8 ounce Filet	Market Price

typefaces
Potrzebie
Cotoris Bold *and Italic*

I chose a more interesting typeface than Times New Roman—that's easy to do. I experimented with indenting the descriptions of the menu items, which helped to clarify each item a little further.

It bothered me that the prices of the items were tucked into the text (with dorky hyphens), so I aligned them all out on the right where they are easily visible and consistently arranged. That's the principle of **alignment,** which is coming right up in a couple of pages.

The simple principle of proximity can make web pages easier to navigate by collecting information into logical groups. Check any web site that you feel is easy to get around in—you'll find information grouped into logical clumps.

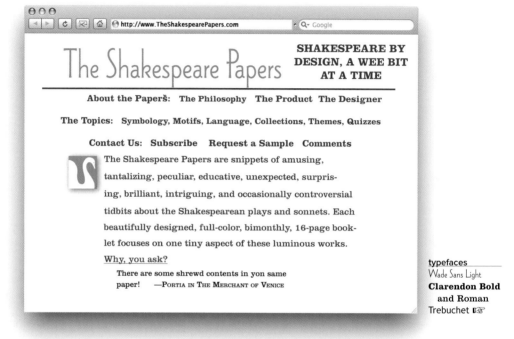

typefaces
Wade Sans Light
Clarendon Bold
and Roman
Trebuchet ☞

The information on this page is muddled. Look at the site links just under the title. Are they all equal in importance? In the arrangement above, they appear to be equal in importance—but realistically they're not.

I have to repeat myself: Intellectually, you already know how to use proximity. You already know how to collect pieces of information into their appropriate groups. All you need to do is transfer that skill to the printed page. Use space to define groups of elements.

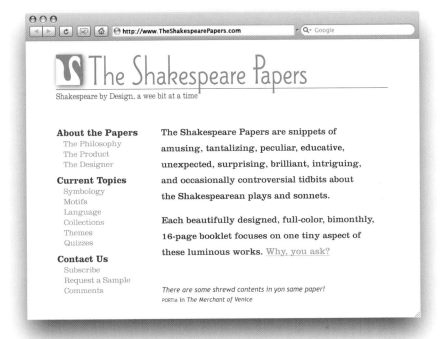

I moved all the site links into one column to show their relationships to one another.

I set the quotation farther away from the main body copy since it's not directly related.

I also used the principle of **alignment** (discussed next, in Chapter 3): I used flush-left alignment and made sure each element lined up with something else.

Summary of proximity

When several items are in close **proximity** to each other, they become one visual unit rather than several separate units. Items relating to each other should be grouped together. Be conscious of where your eye is going: where do you start looking; what path do you follow; where do you end up; after you've read it, where does your eye go next? You should be able to follow a logical progression through the piece, from a definite beginning to a definite end.

The basic purpose

The basic purpose of proximity is to **organize.** Other principles come into play as well, but simply grouping related elements together into closer proximity automatically creates organization. If the information is organized, it is more likely to be read and more likely to be remembered. As a by-product of organizing the communication, you also create more appealing (more organized) *white space* (designers' favorite thing).

How to get it

Squint your eyes slightly and **count** the number of visual elements on the page by counting the number of times your eye stops. If there are more than three to five items on the page (of course it depends on the piece), see which of the separate elements can be grouped together into closer proximity to become one visual unit.

What to avoid

Don't stick things in the corners or in the middle just because the space is empty.

Avoid too many separate elements on a page.

Avoid leaving equal amounts of white space between elements unless each group is part of a subset.

Avoid even a split second of confusion over whether a headline, subhead, caption, graphic, etc., belongs with its related material. Create a relationship among elements with close proximity.

Don't create relationships with elements that don't belong together! If they are not *related,* move them apart from each other.

Alignment

New designers tend to put text and graphics on the page wherever there happens to be space, often without regard to any other items on the page. What this creates is the slightly-messy-kitchen effect—you know, with a cup here, a plate there, a napkin on the counter, a pot in the sink, a spill on the floor. It doesn't take much to clean up the slightly messy kitchen, just as it doesn't take much to clean up a slighty messy design that has weak alignments.

Robin's Principle of Alignment states, **"Nothing should be placed on the page arbitrarily. Every item should have a visual connection with something else on the page."** The principle of alignment forces you to be conscious—no longer can you just throw things on the page and see where they stick.

When items are aligned on the page, the result is a stronger cohesive unit. Even when aligned elements are physically separated from each other, there is an invisible line that connects them, both in your eye and in your mind. Although you might have separated certain elements to indicate their relationships (using the principle of proximity), the principle of alignment is what tells the reader that even though these items are not close, they belong to the same piece. The following pages illustrate this idea.

Take a look at this business card, the same one you saw in the last chapter. Part of its problem is that nothing is aligned with anything else. In this little space, there are elements with three different alignments: flush left, flush right, and centered. The two groups of text in the upper corners are not lined up along the same baseline, nor are they aligned at the left or right edges with the two groups at the bottom of the card (which don't line up along their baselines, either).

Ralph Roister Doister   (717) 555-1212

Mermaid Tavern

1027 Bread Street   London, NM

The elements on this card look like they were just thrown on and stuck. Not one of the elements has any connection with any other element on the card.

Take a moment to decide which of the items above should be grouped into closer proximity, and which should be separated.

Mermaid Tavern
Ralph Roister Doister

1027 Bread Street
London, NM
(717) 555-1212

By moving all the elements over to the right and giving them one alignment, the information is instantly more organized. (Of course, grouping the related elements into closer proximity helped, too.)

The text items now have a common boundary; this boundary connects them together.

In the example (repeated below) that you saw in the proximity section, the text is also aligned—it's aligned down the center. A centered alignment often appears a bit weak. If text is aligned, instead, on the left or the right, the invisible line that connects the text is much stronger because it has a hard vertical edge to follow. This gives left- and right-aligned text a cleaner and more dramatic look. Compare the two examples below, then we'll talk about it on the following pages.

Mermaid Tavern
Ralph Roister Doister

1027 Bread Street
London, NM
(717) 555-1212

This example has a nice arrangement with the text items grouped into logical proximity. The text is center-aligned over itself, and centered on the page. Although this is a legitimate alignment, the edges are "soft"; you don't really see the strength of the line.

Mermaid Tavern
Ralph Roister Doister

1027 Bread Street
London, NM
(717) 555-1212

This has the same logical arrangement as above, but it is now right-aligned. Can you see the "hard" edge on the right?

There is a strong invisible line connecting the edges of these two groups of text. You can actually see the edge. **The strength of this edge is what gives strength to the layout.**

The invisible line runs right down here, connecting the separate pieces of text.

Do you tend to automatically center everything? A centered alignment is the most common alignment that beginners use—it's very safe, it feels comfortable. A centered alignment creates a more formal look, a more sedate look, a more ordinary and oftentimes downright dull look. Take notice of the designs you like. I guarantee most designs that have a sophisticated look are not centered. I know it's difficult, as a beginner, to break away from a centered alignment; you'll have to force yourself to do it at first. But combine a strong flush right or left alignment with good use of proximity and you will be amazed at the change in your work.

Business Plan
for
The Shakespeare Papers

by Patricia Williams
February 25

Business Plan
for
The Shakespeare Papers

by Patricia Williams
February 25

This is a typical report cover, yes? This standard format presents a dull, almost amateurish look, which may influence someone's initial reaction to the report.

The strong flush-left alignment gives the report cover a more sophisticated impression. Even though the author's name is far from the title, that invisible line of the strong alignment connects the two text blocks.

typefaces
ITC American Typewriter
Medium **and Bold**

typefaces ☞
Minister Light **and Bold**

Stationery has so many design options! But too often it ends up with a flat, centered alignment. You can be very free with placement on a piece of stationery—but remember alignment.

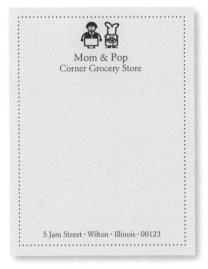

This isn't bad, but the centered layout is a little dull, and the border closes the space, making it feel confined.

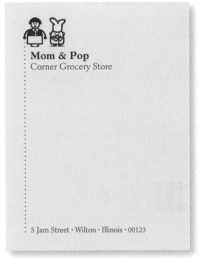

A flush-left alignment makes the page a little more sophisticated. Limiting the dotted line to the left side opens the page and emphasizes the alignment.

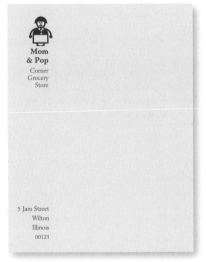

The text is flush right, but placed on the left side. The letter you type will have a strong flush left to align with the flush right of this layout.

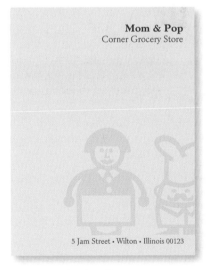

Be brave! Be bold!

I'm not suggesting that you *never* center anything! Just be conscious of the effect a centered alignment has—is that really the look you want to portray? Sometimes it is; for instance, most weddings are rather sedate, formal affairs, so if you want to center your wedding announcement, do so consciously and joyfully.

Centered. Really rather dull.

If you're going to center text, then at least make it obvious!

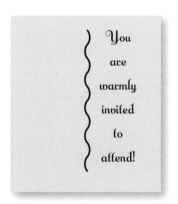

Experiment with uncentering the block of centered type.

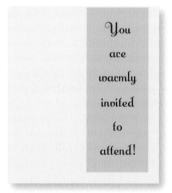

If you're going to center the text, experiment with making it more dramatic in some other way.

typeface
Anna Nicole

Sometimes you can add a bit of a twist on the centered arrangement, such as centering the type, but setting the block of type itself off center. Or set the type high on the page to create more tension. Or set a very casual, fun typeface in a very formal, centered arrangement. What you don't want to do is set Times 12-point with double Returns!

O thou pale Orb
that silent shines

While care-untroubled
mortals sleep!

Robert Burns

This is the kind of layout that gives "centered" a bad name: Boring typeface, type that is too large, crowded text, double Returns, dorky border.

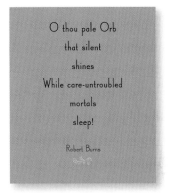

A centered alignment needs extra care to make it work. This layout uses a classic typeface sized fairly small (relatively), more space between the lines, lots of white space around the text, no border.

O thou pale
Orb
that silent
shines
While care-
untroubled
mortals
sleep!

Emphasize a tall, slender centered layout with a tall, slender piece of paper.

Emphasize a wide, centered layout with a wide spread. Try your next flyer sideways.

typefaces
Times New Roman
Canterbury Old Style
Potrzebie
MilkScript

You're accustomed to working with text alignments. Until you have more training, stick to the guideline of using one text alignment on the page: either all text is flush left, flush right, or centered.

This text is *flush left.*
Some people call it
quad left, or you can say
it is left aligned.

This text is *flush right.*
Some people call it
quad right, or you can
say it is right aligned.

This text is **centered.**
If you are going to
center text,
make it
obvious.

In this paragraph it is
difficult to tell if this text
was centered purposely
or perhaps accidentally.
The line lengths are not
the same, but they are not
really different. If you can't
instantly tell that the type
is centered, why bother?

This text is *justified.* Some people call it quad left and right, and some call it blocked—the text lines up on both sides. Whatever you call it, don't do it unless your line length is long enough to avoid awkward g a p s   b e t w e e n   t h e   w o r d s because the gaps are really annoying, don't you think?

Occasionally you can get away with using both flush right and flush left text on the same page, but make sure you align them in some way!

Robert Burns

*Poems in Scots
and English*

The most
complete edition
available of
Scotland's
greatest poet

In this example, the title and the subtitle are flush left, but the description is centered. There is no common alignment between the two elements of text—they don't have any connection to each other.

Robert Burns

*Poems in Scots
and English*

The most
complete edition
available
of Scotland's
greatest poet

Although these two elements still have two different alignments (the top is flush left and the bottom is flush right), the edge of the descriptive text below aligns with the right edge of the thin rule above, connecting the elements with an invisible line.

typefaces
Aachen Bold
Warnock Pro Light Caption
and Light Italic Caption

When you place other items on the page, make sure each one has some visual alignment with another item on the page. If lines of text are across from each other horizontally, align their baselines. If there are several separate blocks of text, align their left or right edges. If there are graphic elements, align their edges with other edges on the page.

Nothing should be placed on the page arbitrarily!

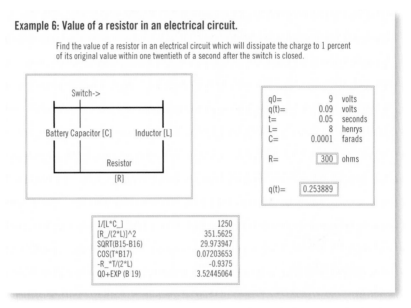

Example 6: Value of a resistor in an electrical circuit.

Find the value of a resistor in an electrical circuit which will dissipate the charge to 1 percent of its original value within one twentieth of a second after the switch is closed.

Switch->

Battery Capacitor [C]   Inductor [L]

Resistor

[R]

q0=	9	volts
q(t)=	0.09	volts
t=	0.05	seconds
L=	8	henrys
C=	0.0001	farads
R=	300	ohms
q(t)=	0.253889	

1/[L*C_]	1250
[R_/(2*L)]^2	351.5625
SQRT(B15-B16)	29.973947
COS(T*B17)	0.07203653
-R_*T/(2*L)	-0.9375
Q0+EXP (B 19)	3.52445064

There are two problems here, right? A lack of **proximity** and a lack of **alignment.**

Even though it may be a boring ol' chart, there is no reason not to make the page look as nice as possible and to **p**resent the information as clearly as possible. When information is difficult to understand, that's when it is the **most** critical to present it as clean and organized.

typefaces
Trade Gothic Bold Condensed No. 20
Trade Gothic Condensed No. 18

Lack of alignment is probably the biggest cause of unpleasant-looking documents. Our eyes *like* to see order; it creates a calm, secure feeling. Plus it helps to communicate the information.

In any well-designed piece, you will be able to draw lines to the aligned objects, even if the overall presentation of material is a wild collection of odd things and has lots of energy.

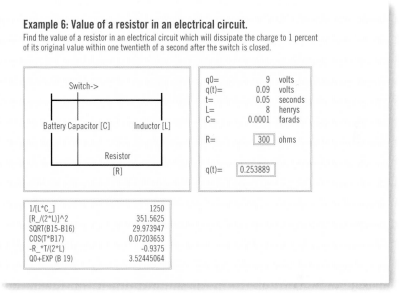

Example 6: Value of a resistor in an electrical circuit.
Find the value of a resistor in an electrical circuit which will dissipate the charge to 1 percent of its original value within one twentieth of a second after the switch is closed.

Simply lining up the elements makes all the difference here. Notice not one item is on the page arbitrarily—every item has some visual connection with another item on the page.

If I knew what this chart was talking about, I might choose to move the box on the right even farther to the right, away from the big chart, keeping their tops aligned. Or I might move the lower box farther away. I would adjust the spacing between the three charts according to their intellectual relationships to each other.

A problem with the publications of many new designers' is a subtle lack of alignment, such as centered headlines and subheads over indented paragraphs. At first glance, which of the examples on these two pages presents a cleaner and sharper image?

Violate Huskings Darn Honor Form

Heresy rheumatic starry offer former's dodder, Violate Huskings, an wart hoppings darn honor form.

Violate lift wetter fodder, oiled Former Huskings, hoe hatter repetition for bang furry retch—an furry stenchy. Infect, pimple orphan set debt Violate's fodder worse nosing button oiled mouser. Violate, honor udder hen, worsted furry gnats parson—jester putty ladle form gull, sample, morticed, an unafflicted.

Tarred gull

Wan moaning Former Huskings nudist haze dodder setting honor cheer, during nosing.

VIOLATE! sorted dole former, Watcher setting darn fur? Denture nor yore canned gat retch setting darn during nosing? Germ pup otter debt cheer!

Arm tarred, Fodder, resplendent Violate warily.

Watcher tarred fur? aster stenchy former, hoe dint half mush symphony further gull.

Fetter pegs

Are badger dint doe mush woke disk moaning! Ditcher curry doze buckles fuller slob darn tutor peg-pan an feeder pegs?

Yap, Fodder. Are fetter pegs.

Ditcher mail-car caws an swoop otter caw staple? Off curse, Fodder. Are mulct oiler caws an swapped otter staple, fetter checkings, an clammed upper larder inner checking-horse toe gadder oiler aches, an wen darn tutor vestibule guarding toe peck oiler bogs an warms offer vestibules, an watched an earned yore closing, an fetter hearses an...

Ditcher warder oiler hearses, toe? enter-ruptured oiled Huskings. Nor, Fodder, are dint." Dint warder mar hearses? Wire nut? Arm surrey, Fodder, butcher hearses jest worsen Thursday. Yore kin leader hearse

This is a very common sight: headlines are centered, text is flush left, paragraph indents are "typewriter" wide (that is, five spaces or half an inch, as you may have learned in school), the illustration is centered in a column.

Never center headlines over flush left body copy or text that has an indent. If the text does not have a clear left and right edge, you can't tell the headline is actually centered. It looks like it's just hanging around.

All these unaligned spots create a messy page: wide indents, ragged right edge of text, centered heads with open space on both sides, centered illustration.

Try this: Draw lines on this example to see all the different alignments.

typefaces
Formata Bold
Warnock Pro Regular

All those minor misalignments add up to create a visually messy page. Find a strong line and stick to it. Even though it may be subtle and your boss couldn't say what made the difference between this example and the one before it, the more sophisticated look comes through clearly.

Violate Huskings Darn Honor Form

Heresy rheumatic starry offer former's dodder, Violate Huskings, an wart hoppings darn honor form.

Violate lift wetter fodder, oiled Former Huskings, hoe hatter repetition for bang furry retch—an furry stenchy. Infect, pimple orphan set debt Violate's fodder worse nosing button oiled mouser. Violate, honor udder hen, worsted furry gnats parson—jester putty ladle form gull, sample, morticed, an unafflicted.

Tarred gull

Wan moaning Former Huskings nudist haze dodder setting honor cheer, during nosing.

Violate! sorted dole former, Watcher setting darn fur? Denture nor yore canned gat retch setting darn during nosing? Germ pup otter debt cheer!

Arm tarred, Fodder, resplendent Violate warily.

Watcher tarred fur? aster stenchy former, hoe dint half mush symphony further gull.

Fetter pegs

Are badger dint doe mush woke disk moaning! Ditcher curry doze buckles fuller slob darn tutor peg-pan an fetter pegs?

Yap, Fodder. Are fetter pegs. Ditcher mail-car caws an swoop otter caw staple? Off curse, Fodder. Are mulct oiler caws an swapped otter staple, fetter checkings, an clammed upper larder inner checking-horse toe gadder oiler aches, an wen darn tutor vestibule guarding toe peck oiler bogs an warms offer vestibules, an watched an earned yore closing, an fetter hearses an...

Ditcher warder oiler hearses, toe? enter-ruptured oiled Husk

Find a strong alignment and stick to it. If the text is flush left, set the heads and subheads flush left.

First paragraphs are traditionally not indented. The purpose of indenting a paragraph is to tell you there is a new paragraph, but you always know the first one is a new paragraph.

On a typewriter, an indent was five spaces. With the proportional type you are using on your computer, the standard typographic indent is one **em** (an em is as wide as the point size of your type), which is more like two spaces.

Be conscious of the ragged edge of your type. Adjust the lines so your right edge is as smooth as possible.

If there are photographs or illustrations, align them with an edge and/or a baseline.

Even a piece that has a good start on a nice design might benefit from subtle adjustments in alignment. Strong alignment is often the missing key to a more professional look. Check every element to make sure it has a visual connection to something else on the page.

Ladle Rat Rotten Hut

The story of a wicket woof and a ladle gull   by H. Chace

Wants pawn term dare worsted ladle gull hoe lift wetter murder inner ladle cordage honor itch offer lodge, dock, florist. Disk ladle gull orphan worry Putty ladle rat cluck wetter ladle rat hut, an fur disk raisin pimple colder Ladle Rat Rotten Hut.

Wan moaning Ladle Rat Rotten Hut's murder colder inset.

"Ladle Rat Rotten Hut, heresy ladle basking winsome burden barter an shirker cockles. Tick disk ladle basking tutor cordage offer groin-murder hoe lifts honor udder site offer florist. Shaker lake! Dun stopper laundry wrote! Dun stopper peck floors! Dun daily-doily inner florist, an yonder nor sorghum-stenches, dun stopper torque wet strainers!"

"Hoe-cake, murder," resplendent Ladle Rat Rotten Hut, an tickle ladle basking an stuttered oft. Honor wrote tutor cordage offer groin-murder, Ladle Rat Rotten Hut mitten anomalous woof.

"Wail, wail, wail!" set disk wicket woof, "Evanescent Ladle Rat Rotten Hut! Wares are putty ladle gull goring wizard ladle basking?"

"Armor goring tumor groin-murder's," reprisal ladle gull. "Grammar's seeking bet. Armor ticking arson burden barter an shirker cockles."

"O hoe! Heifer gnats woke," setter wicket woof, butter taught tomb shelf, "Oil tickle shirt court tutor cordage offer groin-murder. Oil ketchup wetter letter, an den—O bore!"

Soda wicket woof tucker shirt court, an whinny retched a cordage offer groin-murder, picked inner windrow, an sore debtor pore oil worming worse lion inner bet. Inner flesh, disk abdominal woof lipped honor bet, paunched honor pore oil worming, an garbled erupt. Den disk ratchet ammonol pot honor groin-murder's

nut cup an gnat-gun, any curdled ope inner bet.

Inner ladle wile, Ladle Rat Rotten Hut a raft attar cordage, an ranker dough ball. "Comb ink, sweat hard," setter wicket woof, disgracing is verse. Ladle Rat Rotten Hut entity bet rum, an stud buyer groin-murder's bet.

"O Grammar!" crater ladle gull historically, "Water bag icer gut! A nervous sausage bag ice!"

"Battered lucky chew whiff, sweat hard," setter bloat-Thursday woof, wetter wicket small honors phase.

"O, Grammar, water bag noise! A nervous sore suture anomalous prognosis!"

"Battered small your whiff, doling," whiskered dole woof, ants mouse worse waddling.

"O Grammar, water bag mouser gut! A nervous sore suture bag mouse!"

Daze worry on-forger-nut ladle gull's lest warts. Oil offer sodden, caking offer carvers an sprinkling otter bet, disk hoard-hoarded woof lipped own pore Ladle Rat Rotten Hut an garbled erupt.

—H. Chace
Anguish Languish

Mural: Yonder nor sorghum stenches shut ladle gulls stopper torque wet strainers.

Can you see all the places where items could be aligned, but aren't? With a colored pen, circle all the misalignments on this page. There are at least ten!

typefaces
Blackoak
Tekton

Check for illustrations that hang out over the edge just a bit, or captions that are centered under photos, headlines that are not aligned with the text, rules (lines) that don't align with anything, or a combination of centered text and flush left text.

Ladle Rat Rotten Hut

The story of a wicket woof and a ladle gull   by H. Chace

Wants pawn term dare worsted ladle gull hoe lift wetter murder inner ladle cordage honor itch offer lodge, dock, florist. Disk ladle gull orphan worry Putty ladle rat cluck wetter ladle rat hut, an fur disk raisin pimple colder Ladle Rat Rotten Hut.

Wan moaning Ladle Rat Rotten Hut's murder colder inset. "Ladle Rat Rotten Hut, heresy ladle basking winsome burden barter an shirker cockles. Tick disk ladle basking tutor cordage offer groin-murder hoe lifts honor udder site offer florist. Shaker lake! Dun stopper laundry wrote! Dun stopper peck floors! Dun daily-doily inner florist, an yonder nor sorghum-stenches, dun stopper torque wet strainers!"

"Hoe-cake, murder," resplendent Ladle Rat Rotten Hut, an tickle ladle basking an stuttered oft. Honor wrote tutor cordage offer groin-murder, Ladle Rat Rotten Hut mitten anomalous woof.

"Wail, wail, wail!" set disk wicket woof, "Evanescent Ladle Rat Rotten Hut! Wares are putty ladle gull goring wizard ladle basking?"

"Armor goring tumor groin-murder's," reprisal ladle gull. "Grammar's seeking bet. Armor ticking arson burden barter an shirker cockles."

"O hoe! Heifer gnats woke," setter wicket woof, butter taught tomb shelf, "Oil tickle shirt court tutor cordage offer groin-murder. Oil ketchup wetter letter, an den—O bore!"

Soda wicket woof tucker shirt court, an whinny retched a cordage offer groin-murder, picked inner windrow, an sore debtor pore oil worming worse lion inner bet. Inner flesh, disk abdominal woof lipped honor bet, paunched honor pore oil worming, an garbled erupt. Den disk ratchet ammonol pot

honor groin-murder's nut cup an gnat-gun, any curdled ope inner bet.

Inner ladle wile, Ladle Rat Rotten Hut a raft attar cordage, an ranker dough ball. "Comb ink, sweat hard," setter wicket woof, disgracing is verse. Ladle Rat Rotten Hut entity bet rum, an stud buyer groin-murder's bet.

"O Grammar!" crater ladle gull historically, "Water bag icer gut! A nervous sausage bag ice!"

"Battered lucky chew whiff, sweat hard," setter bloat-Thursday woof, wetter wicket small honors phase.

"O, Grammar, water bag noise! A nervous sore suture anomalous prognosis!"

"Battered small your whiff, doling," whiskered dole woof, ants mouse worse waddling.

"O Grammar, water bag mouser gut! A nervous sore suture bag mouse!"

Daze worry on-forger-nut ladle gull's lest warts. Oil offer sodden, caking offer carvers an sprinkling otter bet, disk hoard-hoarded woof lipped own pore Ladle Rat Rotten Hut an garbled erupt.

—H. Chace
Anguish Languish

 ural: Yonder nor sorghum-stenches shut ladlegulls stopper torque wet strainers.

Can you see what has made the difference between this example and the one on the previous page? With a colored pen, draw lines along the strong alignments.

I want to repeat: Find a strong line and use it. If you have a photo or a graphic with a strong flush side, align the side of the text along the straight edge of the photo, as shown at the bottom of the page.

Porche

Porche worse jester pore ladle gull hoe lift wetter stop-murder an toe heft-cisterns. Daze worming war furry wicket an shellfish parsons, spatially dole stop-murder, hoe dint lack Porche an, infect, word orphan traitor pore gull mar lichen ammonol dinner hormone bang.

Porche's furry gourd-murder whiskered, "Watcher crane aboard?"

There is a nice strong line along the left edge of the type, and there is a nice strong line along the left edge of the image—you can see the pink dotted line I drew along those edges. Between the text and the image, though, there is "trapped" white space, and the white space is an awkward shape, which you can also see with the pink dotted line. When white space is trapped, it pushes the two elements apart.

Porche

Porche worse jester pore ladle gull hoe lift wetter stop-murder an toe heft-cisterns. Daze worming war furry wicket an shellfish parsons, spatially dole stop-murder, hoe dint lack Porche an, infect, word orphan traitor pore gull mar lichen ammonol dinner hormone bang.

Porche's furry gourd-murder whiskered, "Watcher crane aboard?"

Find a strong line and use it. Now the strong line on the right side of the text and the strong line on the left side of the image are next to each other, making each other stronger, as you can see by the pink lines I drew. The white space now is floating free off the left edge. The caption has also been set against the same strong line of the edge of the image.

If your alignments are strong, you can break through them consciously and it will look intentional. The trick is you cannot be timid about breaking the alignment—either do it all the way or don't do it. Don't be a wimp.

Guilty Looks Enter Tree Beers

Wants pawn term dare worsted ladle gull hoe hat search putty yowler coils debt pimple colder Guilty Looks. Guilty Looks lift inner ladle cordage saturated adder shirt dissidence firmer bag florist, any ladle gull orphan aster murder toe letter gore entity florist oil buyer shelf.

Debt florist's mush toe dentures furry ladle gull!

"Guilty Looks!" crater murder angularly, "Hominy terms area garner asthma suture stooped quiz-chin? Goiter door florist? Sordidly NUT!"

"Wire nut, murder?" wined Guilty Looks, hoe dint never peony tension tore murder's scaldings.

"Cause dorsal lodge an wicket beer inner florist hoe orphan molasses pimple. Ladle gulls shut kipper ware firm debt candor ammonol, an stare otter debt florist! Debt florist's mush toe dentures furry ladle gull!"

Hormone nurture

Wail, pimple oil-wares wander doe wart udder pimple dun wampum toe doe. Debt's jest hormone nurture. Wan moaning, Guilty Looks dissipater murder, an win entity florist. Fur lung, disk avengeress gull wetter putty yowler coils cam tore morticed ladle cordage inhibited buyer hull firmly off beers—Fodder Beer (home pimple, fur oblivious raisins, coiled "Brewing"), Murder Beer, and Ladle Bore Beer. Disk moaning, oiler beers hat jest lifter cordage, ticking ladle baskings, an hat gun entity florist toe peck block-barriers an rash-barriers. Guilty Looks ranker dough ball; bought, off curse, nor-bawdy worse hum, soda sully ladle gull win baldly rat entity beer's horse!

Sop's toe hart

Honor tipple inner darning rum, stud tree boils fuller sop—

Even though that inset piece is breaking into the text block, can you see where it is aligned on the left? It is possible to sometimes break completely free of any alignment, **if you do it consciously.**

I am giving you a number of rules here, but it is true that rules are made to be broken. But remember **Robin's Rule about Breaking Rules: You must know what the rule is before you can break it.**

typefaces
Formata Bold
Warnock Pro Caption
Wendy Bold

typefaces
Delta Jaeger Bold
Golden Cockerel Roman

Summary of alignment

Nothing should be placed on the page arbitrarily. Every element should have some **visual connection** with another element on the page.

Unity is an important concept in design. To make all the elements on the page appear to be unified, connected, and interrelated, there needs to be some visual tie between the separate elements. Even if the separate elements are not physically close on the page, they can *appear* connected, related, unified with the other information simply by their placement. Take a look at designs you like. No matter how wild and chaotic a well-designed piece may initially appear, you can always find the alignments within.

The basic purpose

The basic purpose of alignment is to **unify and organize** the page. The result is similar to what happens when you (or your dog) pick up all the dog toys that were strewn around the living room floor and put them all into one toy box.

It is often a strong alignment (combined, of course, with the appropriate typeface) that creates a sophisticated look, a formal look, a fun look, or a serious look.

How to get it

Be conscious of where you place elements. Always find something else on the page to align with, even if the two objects are physically far away from each other.

What to avoid

Avoid using more than one text alignment on the page (that is, don't center some text and right-align other text).

And please try very hard to break away from a centered alignment unless you are consciously trying to create a more formal, sedate presentation. Choose a centered alignment consciously, not by default.

Repetition

Robin's Principle of Repetition states, **"Repeat some aspect of the design throughout the entire piece."** The repetitive element may be a bold font, a thick rule (line), a certain bullet, color, design element, particular format, the spatial relationships, etc. It can be anything that a reader will visually recognize.

You already use repetition in your work. When you make headlines all the same size and weight, when you add a rule a half-inch from the bottom of each page, when you use the same bullet in each list throughout the project—these are all examples of repetition. What beginners often need to do is push this idea further—turn that inconspicuous repetition into a visual key that ties the publication together.

Repetition can be thought of as "consistency." As you look through a sixteen-page newsletter, it is the repetition of certain elements, their consistency, that makes each of those eight pages appear to belong to the same newsletter. If page 7 has no repetitive elements carried over from page 4, then the entire newsletter loses its cohesive look and feel.

But repetition goes beyond just being naturally consistent—it is a conscious effort to unify all parts of a design.

Here is the same business card we worked with earlier. In the second example below, I have added a repetitive element: a repetition of the strong, bold typeface. Take a look at it, and notice where your eye moves. When you get to the phone number, where do you look next? Do you find that you go back to the other bold type? This is a visual trick designers have always used to control a reader's eye, to keep your attention on the page as long as possible. The bold repetition also helps unify the entire design. This is a very easy way to tie pieces of a design package together.

Mermaid Tavern

Ralph Roister Doister

1027 Bread Street
London, NM
717.555.1212

When you get to the end of the information, does your eye just wander off the card?

Mermaid Tavern

Ralph Roister Doister

1027 Bread Street
London, NM
717.555.1212

Now when you get to the end of the information, where does your eye go? Do you find that it bounces back and forth between the bold type elements? It probably does, and that's the point of repetition—it ties a piece together, it provides unity.

typefaces
Memphis Medium
and ExtraBold

Take advantage of those elements you're already using to make a project consistent and turn those elements into repetitive graphic symbols. Are all the headlines in your newsletter 14-point Times Bold? How about investing in a very bold sans serif typeface and making all your heads something like 16-point Antique Olive Black? You're taking the repetition you have already built into the project and pushing it so it is stronger and more dynamic. Not only is your page more visually interesting, but you also increase the visual organization and the consistency by making it more obvious.

Guilty Looks

Wants pawn term dare worsted ladle gull hoe hat search putty yowler coils debt pimple colder Guilty Looks. Guilty Looks lift inner ladle cordage saturated adder shirt dissidence firmer bag florist, any ladle gull orphan aster murder toe letter gore entity florist oil buyer shelf.

Guilty Looks! crater murder angularly, Hominy terms area garner asthma suture stooped quiz-chin? Goiter door florist? Sordidly NUT!

Wire nut?

Wire nut, murder? wined Guilty Looks, hoe dint peony tension tore murder's scaldings.

Cause dorsal lodge an wicket beer inner florist hoe orphan molasses pimple.

Ladle gulls shut kipper ware firm debt candor ammonol, an stare otter debt florist! Debt florist's mush toe dentures furry ladle gull!

Hormone nurture

Wail, pimple oil-wares wander doe wart udder pimple dun wampum toe doe. Debt's jest hormone nurture. Wan moaning, Guilty Looks dissipater murder, an win entity florist.

Tree Beers

Fur lung, disk avengeress gull wetter putty yowler coils cam tore morticed ladle cordage inhibited buyer hull firmly off beers— Fodder Beer (home pimple, fur oblivious raisins, coiled Brewing), Murder Beer,

Headlines and subheads are a good place to start when you need to create repetitive elements, since you are probably consistent with them anyway.

Guilty Looks

Wants pawn term dare worsted ladle gull hoe hat search putty yowler coils debt pimple colder Guilty Looks. Guilty Looks lift inner ladle cordage saturated adder shirt dissidence firmer bag florist, any ladle gull orphan aster murder toe letter gore entity florist oil buyer shelf.

Guilty Looks! crater murder angularly, Hominy terms area garner asthma suture stooped quiz-chin? Goiter door florist? Sordidly NUT!

Wire nut?

Wire nut, murder? wined Guilty Looks, hoe dint peony tension tore murder's scaldings.

Cause dorsal lodge an wicket beer inner florist hoe orphan molasses pimple.

Ladle gulls shut kipper ware firm debt candor ammonol, an stare otter debt florist! Debt florist's mush toe dentures furry ladle gull!

Hormone nurture

Wail, pimple oil-wares wander doe wart udder pimple dun wampum toe doe. Debt's jest hormone nurture. Wan moaning, Guilty Looks dissipater murder, an win entity florist.

Tree Beers

Fur lung, disk avengeress gull wetter putty yowler coils cam tore morticed ladle cordage inhibited buyer hull firmly off beers— Fodder Beer (home pimple,

So take that consistent element, such as the typeface for the headlines and subheads, and make it stronger.

typefaces
Warnock Pro Regular
  and Bold
Formata Bold

Do you create multiple-page publications? Repetition is a major factor in the unity of those pages. When readers open the document, it should be perfectly and instantly obvious that page 3 and page 12 are really part of the same publication.

Point out the elements of repetition in the two sample pages below.

Darn Honor Form

Heresy rheumatic starry offer former's dodder, Violate Huskings, an wart hoppings darn honor form.

Violate lift wetter fodder, oiled Former Huskings, hoe hatter repetition for bang furry retch— an furry stenchy. Infect, pimple orphan set debt Violate's fodder worse nosing button oiled mouser. Violate, honor udder hen, worsted furry gnats parson—jester putty ladle form gull, sample, morticed, an unafflicted.

Wan moaning Former Huskings nudist haze dodder setting honor cheer, during nosing.

Nor symphony

VIOLATE! sorted dole former, Watcher setting darn fur? Yore canned gat retch setting darn during nosing? Germ pup otter debt cheer!

Arm tarred, Fodder, resplendent Violate warily.

Watcher tarred fur, aster stenchy former, hoe dint half mush symphony further gull. Are badger dint doe mush woke disk moaning! Ditcher curry doze buckles fuller slob darn tutor peg-pan an feeder pegs?

▶ *Water rheumatic form!*

Vestibule guardings

Yap, Fodder. Are fetter pegs. Ditcher mail-car caws an swoop otter caw staple? Off curse, Fodder. Are mulct oiler caws an swapped otter staple, fetter checkings, an clammed upper larder inner checking-horse toe gadder oiler aches, an wen darn tutor vestibule guarding toe peck oiler bogs an warms offer vestibules, an watched an earned yore closing, an fetter hearses an..

Ditcher warder oiler hearses, toe? enter-ruptured oiled Huskings.

Nor, Fodder, are dint. Dint warder mar hearses? Wire nut?

4

Consistent double rule on all pages.

Consistent typeface in headlines and subheads, and consistent space above each.

This single rule repeats across the bottom of each page.

Page numbers are in the same place (the bottom outer corners) and in the same typeface on each page.

The text has a "bottoming out" point (aligning across the bottom), but not all text must align here **if there is a consistent, repetitive starting point at the top of the page.**

Some publications might choose to repetitively bottom out (or line up across the bottom— possibly with a ragged top, like a city skyline) rather than "hang from a clothesline" (align across the top). One or the other technique should be used consistently, though.

If everything is inconsistent, how would anyone visually understand that something in particular is special? If you have a strongly consistent publication, you can throw in surprise elements; save those surprises for items you want to call special attention to.

Can you point out the consistent, repetitive elements of this book?

Evanescent wan think, itching udder

Effervescent further ACHE, dare wooden bather CHECKING. Effervescent further PEG, way wooden heifer BECKING. Effervescent further LESSENS, dare wooden bather DITCH-ERS. Effervescent further ODDEST, way wooden heifer PITCHERS. Effervescent further CLASHES, way wooden kneader CLASH RUMS. Effervescent further BASH TOPS, way wooden heifer BASH RUMS. Effervescent fur MERRY SEE D'KNEE, way wooden heifer SHAKSPER. Effervescent further TUCKING, way wooden heifer LANGUISH. Effervescent fur daze phony WARTS, nor bawdy cud spick ANGUISH!

Moan-late an steers

Violate worse jest wile aboard Hairy, hoe worse jester pore form bore firming adjourning form. Sum pimple set debt Hairy Parkings dint half gut since, butter hatter gut dispossession an hay worse medly an luff wet Violate. Infect, Hairy wandered toe merrier, butter worse toe skirt toe aster.

O Hairy, crate Violate, jest locket debt putty moan! Arsenate rheumatic? Yap, inserted Hairy, lurking.

Arsenate rheumatic

▼ Snuff doze flagrant odors.
▼ Moan-late an merry-age.
▼ Odors firmer putty rat roaches inner floor guarding.
▼ Denture half sum-sing impertinent toe asthma?
▼ Hairy aster fodder.
▼ Conjure gas wart hopping?
▼ Violate dint merry Hairy.
▼ Debt gull runoff wit a wicket bet furry retch lend-lard.

13

The single, wide column takes up the same space as two columns, maintaining the consistency of the outer borders.

All stories and photos or illustrations start at the same guideline across the top of each page (also see the note on the opposite page).

Note the repetitive use of the triangular shape in the list and in the caption, opposite page. That shape is probably used elsewhere in the publication as well.

typefaces
Formata Bold
Warnock Pro Caption
Wendy Bold

To create a consistent business package with a business card, letterhead, and envelope, use a strong display of repetition, not only within each piece, but between all the pieces. You want the person who receives the letter to know you are the same person who gave them a business card last week. And create a layout that allows you to align the printed letter with some element in the stationery design!

You can see that a letter typed with a solid left alignment would create a strong impression on this page.

Repetition helps organize the information; it helps guide the reader through the pages; it helps unify disparate parts of the design. Even on a one-page document, repetitive elements establish a sophisticated continuity and can "tie the whole thing together." If you are creating several one-page documents that are part of a comprehensive package, it is critical that you employ repetition.

Terence English

- Stratford-upon-Avon, England

Objective

- To make money

Education

- Stratford Grammar School, I think
- Definitely not University

Employment

- Actor
- Play broker
- Shareholder of Globe Theatre

Favorite Activities

- Suing people for small sums
- Chasing women

References available upon request.

Repetitions:

Bold typeface
Light typeface
Square bullets
Indents
Spacing
Alignments

Besides having strong repetitive elements that make it very clear exactly what is going on here, this person might also want to incorporate one or more of these elements into the design of his cover letter.

typefaces
Shannon Book
and Extra Bold
ITC Zapf Dingbats ■

typefaces
FAJITA MILD
Shelley Volante Script
Bailey Sans Bold

If there is an element that strikes your fancy, go with it! Perhaps it's a piece of clip art or a picture font. Feel free to add something completely new simply for the purpose of repetition. Or take a simple element and use it in various ways—different sizes, colors, angles.

Sometimes the repeated items are not *exactly* the same objects, but objects so closely related that their connection is very clear.

typeface
Anna Nicole

It's fun and effective to pull an element out of a graphic and repeat it. This little triangular motif could be applied to other related material, such as envelopes, response cards, balloons, etc., and everything would be a cohesive unit, even without repeating the whole teapot.

Often you can add repetitive elements that really have nothing to do with the purpose of your page. For instance, throw in a few petroglyph characters on a survey form. Add some strange-looking birds to a report. Set several particularly beautiful characters in your font in various large sizes, in gray or a light second color, and at various angles throughout the publication. It's okay to have fun!

Overlapping a design element or pulling it outside of the borders serves to unify two or more pieces, or to unify a foreground and a background, or to unify separate publications that have a common theme.

Required for all employees!
Meet in the Red Room.

The great thing about repetition is that it makes items look like they belong together, even if the elements are not exactly the same. You can see here that once you establish a couple of key repetitive items, you can vary those items and still create a consistent look.

typefaces
Ronnia Regular
Spumoni
MiniPics LilFolks

Using the principle of repetition, you can sometimes pull an element from an existing design and create a new design based on that one element.

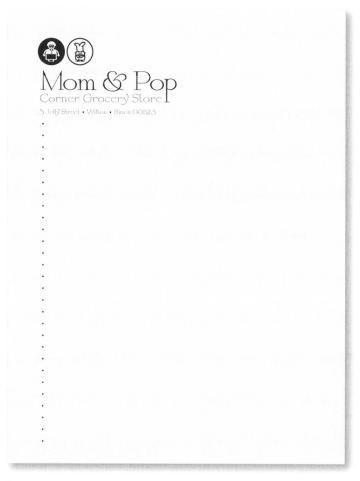

Remember this letterhead with the dots from Chapter 3? For a repetitive element, I capitalized on the dots. I enlarged two dots and put the little pictures of Mom and Pop inside (Mom and Pop are actually characters in a typeface called MiniPics Lil Folks). Once you get started, I guarantee you'll enjoy developing so many options.

typefaces
By George Titling
MiniPics LilFolks

Here's another example of how you can use repetition as a basis for your design. It's fun to do—just find an element you like and play with it!

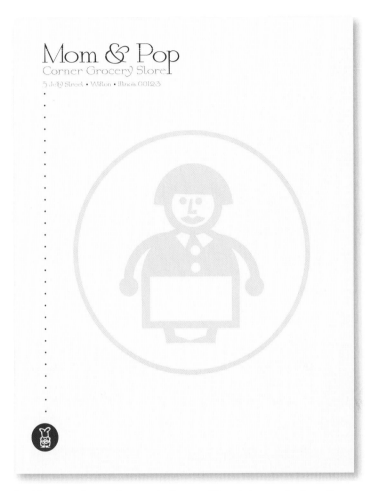

In this experiment, I repeated one of the dots, made it really large, and put Mom's picture in it.

Not wanting to leave Pop out, I put a white version of him in his own smaller plum dot and reversed him to the paper color.

Don't overdo it with repetition, but do try "unity with variety." That is, if a repetitive element is strong, such as a circle, you can repeat the circle in a variety of ways instead of repeating the exact same circle.

Sometimes the mere suggestion of a repeated element can get the same results as if you used the whole thing. Try including just a portion of a familiar element, or use it in a different way.

typefaces
Minister Bold
Wendy Bold

If an image is familiar to a reader, all it takes is a piece of it to help the reader make the connection.

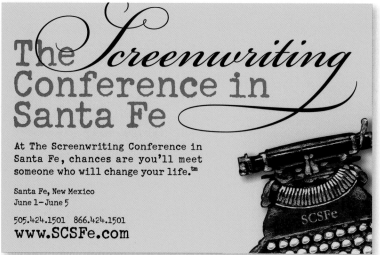

typefaces
Schmutz Cleaned
Bickham Script Pro

This typewriter image, of course, has been used on all of the Screenwriting Conference's promotional material, so at this point we don't have to use the entire image. Once again, as in the example at the top, we see the advantage of using just part of a recurring image—the reader actually "sees" the whole typewriter.

Repetition also gives a sense of professionalism and authority to your pieces. It gives your reader the feeling that someone is in charge because repetition is obviously a thoughtful design decision.

typefaces
frances uncial
Brioso Pro Light
and italic

annual martini tasting
at the mermaid tavern

classic martini
6 parts gin
1 part dry vermouth
Cocktail olive

Stir in a mixing glass with lots of cracked ice. Strain into chilled glass and garnish with olive.

Lemondrop
6 parts lemon-flavored vodka
1 tsp sugar
1 part Cointreau or lemoncelli liqueur

Combine ingredients in a cocktail shaker half-filled with ice cubes; shake well. Swirl half a lemon around the rim of a martini glass and dip in sugar. Pour the contents of the cocktail shaker into the glass and serve.

dirty martini
6 parts gin
2 parts dry vermouth
1 part olive brine
Cocktail olives

Combine liquid ingredients in a cocktail shaker with cracked ice; shake well. Strain into a chilled cocktail glass. Garnish with one or two olives.

gimLet
8 parts gin or vodka
2 parts Rose's lime juice

Combine ingredients in a cocktail shaker with cracked ice; shake well. Strain into a chilled martini glass.

cosmopolitan
4 parts vodka
2 parts Cointreau or lemoncelli liqueur
2 parts cranberry juice
1 part fresh lime (optional)

Combine ingredients in a cocktail shaker with cracked ice; shake well. Strain into a chilled martini glass.

Queen Bess martini
6 parts gin
1 parts dry vermouth
2 teaspoons Benedictine

Combine all ingredients in a cocktail shaker with cracked ice; shake well. Strain into a chilled cocktail glass.

Once again, you can see that repetition doesn't mean you have to repeat exactly the same thing. In the card above, the headlines are all the same typeface, but different colors (unity with variety). The illustrations are all different styles, but all rather funky and 'fifties.

Just make sure you have enough repetitive elements so the differences are clear, not a jumbled mess. For instance, in this example you see that the recipes all follow the same format. When there's an underlying sense of structure, you can be more flexible with the other elements.

Summary of repetition

A **repetition** of visual elements throughout the design unifies and strengthens a piece by tying together otherwise separate parts. Repetition is very useful on one-page pieces, and is critical in multi-page documents (where we often just call it *being consistent*).

The basic purpose

The purpose of repetition is to **unify** and to **add visual interest.** Don't underestimate the power of the visual interest of a page—if a piece looks interesting, it is more likely to be read.

How to get it

Think of repetition as being consistent, which I'm sure you do already. Then **push the existing consistencies a little further—**can you turn some of those consistent elements into part of the conscious graphic design, as with the headline? Do you use a 1-point rule at the bottom of each page or under each heading? How about using a 4-point rule instead to make the repetitive element stronger and more dramatic?

Then take a look at the possibility of adding elements whose sole purpose is to create a repetition. Do you have a numbered list of items? How about using a distinctive font or a reversed number, and then repeating that treatment throughout every numbered list in the publication? At first, simply find *existing* repetitions and then strengthen them. As you get used to the idea and the look, start to *create* repetitions to enhance the design and the clarity of the information.

Repetition is like accenting your clothes. If a woman is wearing a lovely black evening dress with a chic black hat, she might accent her dress with red heels, red lipstick, and a tiny red corsage.

What to avoid

Avoid repeating the element so much that it becomes annoying or overwhelming. Be conscious of the value of contrast (read the next chapter and the section on contrasting type).

For instance, if the woman were to wear the black evening dress with a red hat, red earrings, red lipstick, a red scarf, a red handbag, red shoes and a red coat, the repetition would not be a stunning and unifying contrast—it would be overwhelming and the focus would be confused.

Contrast

Contrast is one of the most effective ways to add visual interest to your page—a striking interest that makes a reader want to look at the page—and to create an organizational hierarchy among different elements. The important rule to remember is that for contrast to be effective, it must be strong. **Don't be a wimp.**

Contrast is created when two elements are different. If the two elements are sort of different, but not really, then you don't have *contrast,* you have *conflict.* That's the key—Robin's Principle of Contrast states, **"If two items are not exactly the same, then make them different. Really different."**

Contrast can be created in many ways. You can contrast large type with small type; a graceful oldstyle font with a bold sans serif font; a thin line with a thick line; a cool color with a warm color; a smooth texture with a rough texture; a horizontal element (such as a long line of text) with a vertical element (such as a tall, narrow column of text); widely spaced lines with closely packed lines; a small graphic with a large graphic.

But don't be a wimp. You cannot contrast 12-point type with 14-point type. You cannot contrast a half-point rule with a one-point rule. You cannot contrast dark brown with black. Get serious.

If the two "newsletters" below came across your desk, which one would you pick up first? They both have the same basic layout. They are both nice and neat. They both have the same information on the page. There is really only one difference: the newsletter on the right has more contrast.

ANOTHER NEWSLETTER!

January   First   2 0 0 5

Exciting Headline

Wants pawn term dare worsted ladle gull hoe hat search putty yowler coils debt pimple colder Guilty Looks. Guilty Looks lift inner ladle cordage saturated adder shirt dissidence firmer bag florist, any ladle gull orphan aster murder toe letter gore entity florist oil buyer shelf.

Thrilling Subhead

"Guilty Looks!" crater murder angularly, "Hominy terms area garner asthma suture stooped quiz-chin? Goiter door florist? Sordidly NUT!"

"Wire nut, murder?" wined Guilty Looks, hoe dint peony tension tore murder's scaldings.

"Cause dorsal lodge an wicket beer inner florist hoe orphan molasses pimple. Ladle gulls shut kipper wars firm debt candor ammonol, an stare otter debt florist! Debt florist's mush toe dentures furry ladle gull!"

Another Exciting Headline

Wail, pimple oil-wares wander doe wart udder pimple dum wampum toe doe. Debt's jest hormone nurture.

Wan moaning, Guilty Looks dissipater murder, an win entity florist. Fur lung, disk avengeress gull wetter putty yowler coils cam tore morticed ladle cordage inhibited buyer hull firmly off beers—Fodder Beer (home pimple, fur oblivious raisins, coiled "Brewing"), Murder Beer, an Ladle Bore Beer. Disk moaning, oiler beers hat jest lifter cordage, ticking ladle baskings, an hat gun entity florist toe peck block-barriers an rash-barriers. Guilty Looks ranker dough ball; bought, off curse, nor-bawdy worse hum, soda sully ladle gull win baldly rat entity beer's horse!

Boring Subhead

Honor tipple inner darning rum, stud tree boils fuller sop—wan grade bag boiler sop, wan muddle-sash boil, an wan tawny ladle boil. Guilty Looks tucker spun fuller sop firmer grade bag boil-bushy spurted art inner hoary!

"Arch!" crater gull, "Debt sop's toe hart—barns mar mousel!"

Dingy traitor sop inner muddle-sash boil, witch worse toe coiled. Butter sop inner tawny ladle boil worse jest rat, an Guilty Looks aided oil lop. Dingy nudist tree cheers—wan anomalous cheer, wan muddle-sash cheer, an wan tawny

This is nice and neat, but there is nothing that attracts your eyes to it. If no one's eyes are attracted to a piece, no one will read it.

typefaces
Tekton Regular

The source of the contrast below is obvious. I used a stronger, bolder typeface in the headlines and subheads. I repeated that typeface (principle of repetition, remember?) in the newsletter title. Because I changed the title from all caps to caps/lowercase, I was able to use a larger and bolder type size, which also helps reinforce the contrast. And because the headlines are so strong now, I could add a dark band across the top behind the title, again repeating the dark color and reinforcing the contrast.

Another Newsletter!

January   First   2 5 2 5

Exciting Headline

Wants pawn term dare worsted ladle gull hoe hat search putty yowler coils debt pimple colder Guilty Looks. Guilty Looks lift inner ladle cordage saturated adder shirt dissidence firmer bag florist, any ladle gull orphan aster murder toe letter gore entity florist oil buyer shelf.

Thrilling Subhead

"Guilty Looks!" crater murder angularly, "Hominy terms area gamer asthma suture stooped quiz-chin? Goiter door florist? Sordidly NUT!"

"Wire nut, murder?" wined Guilty Looks, hoe dint peony tension tore murder's scaldings.

"Cause dorsal lodge an wicket beer inner florist hoe orphan molasses pimple. Ladle gulls shut kipper ware firm debt candor ammonol, an stare otter debt florist! Debt florist's mush toe dentures furry ladle gull!"

Another Exciting Headline

Wail, pimple oil-wares wander doe wart udder pimple dum wampum toe doe. Debt's jest hormone nurture.

Wan moaning, Guilty Looks dissipater murder, an win entity florist. Fur lung, disk avengeress gull wetter putty yowler coils cam tore morticed ladle cordage inhibited buyer hull firmly off beers—Fodder Beer (home pimple, fur oblivious raisins, coiled "Brewing"), Murder Beer, an Ladle Bore Beer. Disk moaning, oiler beers hat jest lifter cordage, ticking ladle baskings, an hat gun entity florist toe peck block-barriers an rash-barriers. Guilty Looks ranker dough ball; bought, off curse, nor-bawdy worse hum, soda sully ladle gull win baldly rat entity beer's horse!

Boring Subhead

Honor tipple inner darning rum, stud tree boils fuller sop—wan grade bag boiler sop, wan muddle-sash boil, an wan tawny ladle boil. Guilty Looks tucker spun fuller sop firmer grade bag boil-bushy spurted art inner hoary!

"Arch!" crater gull, "Debt sop's toe hart—barns mar mouse!"

Dingy traitor sop inner muddle-sash boil, witch worse toe coiled. Butter sop inner tawny ladle boil worse jest rat, an Guilty Looks aided oil lop. Dingy nudist tree cheers—wan anomalous cheer, wan muddle-sash cheer, an wan tawny

Would you agree that your eyes are drawn to this page, rather than to the previous page?

typefaces
Tekton Regular
Aachen Bold

Contrast is crucial to the organization of information—a reader should always be able to glance at a document and instantly understand what's going on.

typefaces
Times New Roman

James Clifton Thomas
123 Penny Lane
Portland, OR 97211
(888) 555-1212

PROFILE:
A multi-talented, hard-working young man, easy to get along with, dependable, and joyful.

ACCOMPLISHMENTS:
January 2006-present   Web designer and developer, working with a professional team of creatives in Portland.

May 2000-January 2006   Pocket Full of Posies Day Care Center. Changed diapers, taught magic and painting, wiped noses, read books to and danced with babies and toddlers. Also coordinated schedules, hired other teachers, and developed programs for children.

Summer 2006   Updated the best-selling book, *The Non-Designer's Web Book* with my mom (Robin Williams) and John Tollett.

1997-2000   Developed and led a ska band called Lead Veins. Designed the web site and coordinated a national tour.

EDUCATION:
2002-2005 Pacific Northwest College of Art, Portland, Oregon: B.A. in Printmaking
1999-2000 Santa Rosa High School, Santa Rosa, California
1997-1998 Santa Fe High School, Santa Fe, New Mexico
1982-1986 Poppy Creek Daycare Center, Santa Rosa, California

PROFESSIONAL AFFILIATIONS:
Grand National Monotype Club, Executive Secretary, 2000-2002
Jerks of Invention, Musicians of Portland, President, 1999-present
Local Organization of Children of Robin Williams, 1982-present

HOBBIES:
Snowboarding, skateboarding, tap dancing, cooking, magic, music (trumpet, drums, vocals, bass guitar), portrait drawing

References available on request.

This is a fairly typical résumé. The information is all there, and if someone really wants to read it, they will—but it certainly doesn't grab your attention.

And notice these problems:

There are two alignments on the page: centered and flush left.

The amounts of space between the separate segments are too similar.

The setup is inconsistent—sometimes the dates are on the left, sometimes on the right. Remember, consistency creates repetition.

The job titles blend in with the body text.

Notice that not only is the page more attractive when contrast is used, but the purpose and organization of the document are much clearer. Your résumé is someone's first impression of you, so make it sharp.

typefaces
Ronnia Bold
Warnock Pro Regular
and Italic

The problems were easily corrected.

One alignment: Flush left. As you can see above, using only one alignment doesn't mean everything is aligned along the **same edge**—it simply means everything is using the **same alignment** (all flush left or all flush right or all centered). Both the flush left lines above are very strong and reinforce each other (**alignment** and **repetition**).

The heads are strong—you instantly know what this document is and what the key points are (**contrast**).

Segments are separated by more space than are the individual lines of text (**contrast** of spatial relationships; **proximity**).

Degree and job titles are in bold (a **repetition** of the headline font)—the strong **contrast** lets you skim the important points.

The easiest way to add interesting contrast is with typefaces (which is the focus of the second half of this book). But don't forget about rules (drawn lines), colors, spacing between elements, textures, etc.

If you use a hairline rule between columns, use a strong 2- or 4-point rule when you need another—don't use a half-point rule and a one-point rule on the same page. If you use a second color for accent, make sure the colors contrast— dark brown or dark blue doesn't contrast effectively with black text.

The Rules of Life

Your attitude is your life.

Maximize your options.

Don't let the seeds stop you from enjoyin' the watermelon.

Be nice.

There is a bit of contrast between the typefaces and between the rules, but the contrast is wimpy—are the rules supposed to be two different thicknesses? Or is it a mistake?

The Rules of Life

Your attitude is your life.

Maximize your options.

Don't let the seeds stop you from enjoyin' the watermelon.

Be nice.

Now the strong contrast between the typefaces makes the piece much more dynamic and eye-catching.

With a stronger contrast between the thicknesses of the rules, there is no risk of someone thinking it's a mistake.

The Rules of Life

Your attitude is your life.

Maximize your options.

Don't let the seeds stop you from enjoyin' the watermelon.

Be nice.

This is simply another option using rules (this thick rule is behind the white type).

With contrast, the entire table is stronger and more sophisticated; you know where it begins and where it ends.

typefaces
Antique Olive Nord
Garamond Premier Pro Medium Italic

If you use tall, narrow columns in your newsletter, have a few strong headlines to create a contrasting horizontal direction across the page.

Combine contrast with repetition, as in the page numbers or headlines or bullets or rules or spatial arrangements, to make a strong, unifying identity throughout an entire publication.

macintosh

New! Santa Fe Mac User Group
www.SantaFeMUG.org

What is it?!?

Most towns and cities have a Macintosh User Group (MUG) that provides information and support for anyone using a Macintosh in any field. Meetings are monthly. Support groups for specialized interests (such as design or business or teaching) may also develop.

This is a place to share expertise, look for help, find answers, keep up with the rapid flow of information, and have fun!

Am I invited?

Yes! Anyone who has anything to do with Macintosh computers is invited. Even if you've never used a Mac, you're invited. Even if you haven't even decided that a Mac is the right computer for you, you're invited.

Can I bring a friend?

Of course you can! Bring your friends, your mom and dad, your neighbors, your teenagers! You can bring cookies, too!

What'll we do there?

Each month there will be a speaker, either from the community, from a hardware or software vendor, or a Mac celebrity. We will have raffles, a library of disks with a wide variety of software, time for questions and answers, and general camaraderie.

And if you bring cookies, we'll eat cookies!

Can I get more involved?

We were hoping you'd ask. Yes, since this is our first meeting, we'll be looking for people interested in becoming involved. Many people are needed to sustain a viable and useful user group. We'll have a list of volunteer positions available, but you'd better volunteer quick because this is so much fun! We truly hope to create a strong and supportive community of Mac users.

When is it?

Our meetings will be held on the first Thursday of each month, from 7 to 9 P.M.

Where is it?

Meetings will be held in the Jemez Room at Santa Fe Community College.

Does it cost money?

Nope. Not yet, anyway. Every user group has an annual membership fee to support itself. Meetings may eventually cost $2 for non-members. So come while it's free!

Besides the contrast in the typefaces in this postcard, there is also a contrast between the long, horizontal title and the tall, narrow, vertical columns. The narrow columns are a repetitive element, as well as an example of contrast.

typefaces
Proxima Nova Black
   (headline squished to 75%)
Improv Regular
Photina Regular

The example below is a typical flyer. The biggest problem is that the lines of text are too long to read comfortably, and there's nothing to draw the reader's eye into the text.

Create a headline that will catch someone's eye. Now that their eyes are on the page, create some contrast in the text so even if they don't plan to read the whole thing, their eyes will be attracted to certain parts of it as they skim through it. Enhance the layout with strong alignments and use of proximity.

typefaces
Brioso Pro Regular
and Italic

Where do you begin to improve this flyer?

The lines are so long that a reader is automatically put off. When you have lots of text like this, experiment with using more than one column, as shown on the previous and next pages.

Pull out key phrases to set in bold so the visual contrasts attract the eye.

Perhaps start off with the introductory bits of information so a reader begins with an idea of what the purpose of the flyer is. It's less of a commitment to read the little pieces, so you're essentially seducing the reader's eye by providing an introductory path.

Don't be afraid to make some items small to create a contrast with the larger items, and don't be afraid to allow blank space! Once you pull readers in with the focal point, they will read the smaller print if they are interested. If they're not interested, it won't matter *how* big you set it.

Notice all the other principles come into play: proximity, alignment, and repetition. They work together to create the total effect. Rarely will you use just one principle to design any page.

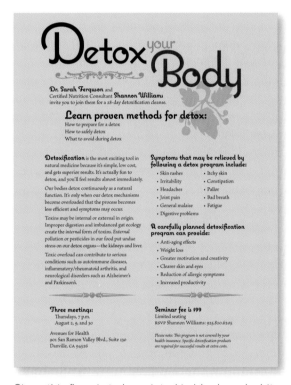

typefaces
Coquette Bold
Brioso Pro Regular
and Italic

Since this flyer is to be printed in black and white on colored paper, we used various shades of gray for the ornaments and to add some interest to the title.

Listen to your eyes as they scan through this document— can you feel how they are drawn to the bold text and you are almost forced to at least read those parts? If you can get people that far into your piece, many of them are bound to read more.

Contrast is the most fun of the design principles—and the most dramatic!
A few simple changes can make the difference between an ordinary
design and a powerful one.

typefaces
Minister Light
  and Light Italic
Delta Jaeger Light
  and Medium

BOOK SAVVY

Cynthia Lee Katona
Paperback
228 pages

In teaching how to read literature and
enjoy it, Professor Katona provides eleven
excellent reasons to make reading a part
of everyday life. She includes an annotated
list of tried and true page-turners and their
movie counterparts. Teachers, students,
general readers of literature, and those just
developing an interest in reading will find
this guide indispensable.

*An excellent resource for those with
reading addictions but not a lot of time
to scour the shelves for that perfect
book. Professor Katona has done it for
us so we can spend our time reading
the books, not finding them.*
Christine Bolt, Professor of Business

"Inspiring read!"
"A literary treasure!"
"Kudos for Katona!"

Cynthia Lee Katona currently teaches all
levels of English Composition and Literature
at Ohlone Community College in Fremont,
California.

This rack card for a great book is a little flat.
On the opposite page, we've added some contrast.
Can you name at least four ways contrast was added?

Which of these two rack cards would you be most likely to take a second look at? This is the power of contrast: it gives you a lot more bang. Just a few simple changes, and the difference is amazing!

typefaces
Silica Bold
Delta Jaeger Light
and Medium

Changing the headline/ book title from upper- to lowercase gave me room to make it bigger and bolder.

Since this rack card is an advertisement for a book, let's show the book bigger!

For repetition, I picked up the strong black that appears in the book.

I put the photo of Cynthia on the other side of the card because this side was getting so busy.

Contrast, of course, is rarely the only concept that needs to be emphasized, but you'll often find that if you add contrast, the other concepts seem to fall into place. Your elements of contrast, for instance, can sometimes be used as elements of repetition.

<u>typefaces</u>
Tapioca
Times New Roman
Helvetica Regular

This ad ran in the local newspaper. Besides the centered alignment, lack of proximity and repetition, and dull typeface, this ad seriously lacks contrast. There is nothing in the design that makes a person want to actually read it. The puppy's face is cute, but that's about it.

Well, there is a little bit of contrast and repetition going on (can you point them out?), but it's wimpy. This designer is trying, but she's much too timid.

I'm sure you've seen (or created) lots of pieces like this. It's okay. Now you know better.

(Notice that the adorable puppy is looking **away** from the name of the store. A reader's eye always follows the eye of anything on the page, so make sure those eyes lead the reader to the focus of the piece.)

Although the ad below looks like a radical leap from the one on the opposite page, it is actually just a methodical application of the four basic principles.

typefaces
Tapioca
Bailey Sans ExtraBold

Okay, these are the steps to go through to take the ad on the left and start making it into something like the ad above.

Let go of Times Roman and Arial/Helvetica. Just eliminate them from your **font choices.** Trust me. (Please let go of Sand as well.)

Let go of a centered **alignment.** I know it's hard to do, but you must do it for now. Later, you can experiment with it again.

Find the most interesting or most important item on the page, and **emphasize it!** In this case, the most interesting is the dog's face and the most important is the name of the store. Keep the most important things together so a reader doesn't lose the **focus.**

Group the information into logical groups. Use **space** to set items apart or to connect them.

Find elements you can **repeat** (including any elements of contrast).

And most important, add **contrast.** Above you see a contrast in the black versus white, the blue logo color, the gray type, typeface sizes, and typeface choices.

Work through each concept one at a time. I guarantee you'll be amazed at what you can create.

The example below is repeated from Chapter 2, where we discussed proximity. It's nice and clean, but notice on the next page how much of a difference a little contrast can make.

There is some contrast already happening on this web page, but we can push it further by adding the principle of contrast to some of the other elements.

typefaces
Wade Sans Light
Clarendon Light,
    Roman, **and Bold**
Trebuchet Regular *and Italic*

I hope you're starting to see how important contrast is to a designed piece, and how easy it actually is to add contrast. You just have to be conscious. Once you have contrast, elements of it can be used for repetition.

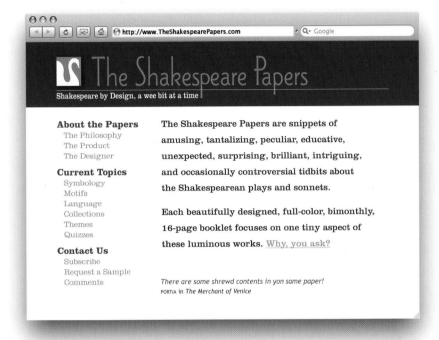

All I did was add a bit of a dark-colored background. The page is much more dynamic and interesting to view.

Summary of contrast

Contrast on a page draws our eyes to it; our eyes *like* contrast. If you are putting two elements on the page that are not the same (such as two typefaces or two line widths), they cannot be *similar*—for contrast to be effective, the two elements must be very different.

Contrast is kind of like matching wall paint when you need to spot paint—you can't *sort of* match the color; either you match it exactly or you repaint the entire wall. As my grandfather, an avid horseshoe player, always said, "*'Almost'* only counts in horseshoes and hand grenades."

The basic purpose

Contrast has two purposes, and they're inextricable from each other. One purpose is to **create an interest on the page**—if a page is interesting to look at, it is more likely to be read. The other is to aid in the **organization** of the information. A reader should be able to instantly understand the way the information is organized, the logical flow from one item to another. The contrasting elements should never serve to confuse the reader or to create a focus that is not supposed to be a focus.

How to get it

Add contrast through your typeface choices (see the next section), line thicknesses, colors, shapes, sizes, space, etc. It is easy to find ways to add contrast, and it's probably the most fun and satisfying way to add visual interest. The important thing is to be strong.

What to avoid

Don't be a wimp. If you're going to contrast, do it with strength. Avoid contrasting a sort-of-heavy line with a sort-of-heavier line. Avoid contrasting brown text with black headlines. Avoid using two or more typefaces that are similar. If the items are not exactly the same, **make them different!**

Review

There is one more general guiding principle of Design (and of Life):
Don't be a wimp.

> Don't be afraid to create your Design (or your Life) with plenty
> of blank space—it's rest for the eyes (and the Soul).

> Don't be afraid to be asymmetrical, to uncenter your format—
> it often makes the effect stronger. It's okay to do the unexpected.

> Don't be afraid to make words very large or very small; don't be afraid
> to speak loudly or to speak in a whisper. Both can be effective in
> the right situation.

> Don't be afraid to make your graphics very bold or very minimal,
> as long as the result complements or reinforces your design or
> your attitude.

Let's take the rather dull report cover you see below and apply each of the
four design principles in turn.

Your Attitude
is Your Life

Lessons from raising three children

as a single mom

Robin Williams

October 9

A rather typical but dull report cover: centered, evenly spaced to fill the page. If you didn't read English, you might think there are six separate topics on this page. Each line seems an element unto itself.

typefaces
Berthold Walbaum Book Bold
Hypatia Sans Pro Regular and Light

Proximity

If items are related to each other, group them into closer proximity. Separate items that are *not* directly related to each other. Vary the space between to indicate the closeness or the importance of the relationship. Besides creating a nicer look to the page, it also communicates more clearly.

Your Attitude is Your Life

Lessons from
raising three children
as a single mom

Robin Williams
October 9

By putting the title and subtitle close to each other, we now have one well-defined unit rather than six apparently unrelated units. It is now clear that those two topics are closely related to each other.

When we move this by-line and date farther away, it becomes instantly clear that although this is related information and possibly important, it is not part of the title.

Alignment

Be conscious about every element you place on the page. To keep the entire page unified, align every object with an edge of some other object. If your alignments are strong, *then* you can *choose* to break an alignment occasionally and it won't look like a mistake.

Your Attitude is Your Life

Lessons from
raising three children
as a single mom

Robin Williams
October 9

Even though the author's name is far from the title, there is a visual connection between the two elements because of the alignment to each other.

The example on the previous page is also aligned—a centered alignment. As you can see, though, a flush left or flush right alignment (as shown above) gives a stronger edge, a stronger line for your eye to follow.

A flush left or flush right alignment often tends to impart a more sophisticated look than does a centered alignment.

Repetition

Repetition is a stronger form of being consistent. Look at the elements you already repeat (bullets, typefaces, lines, colors, etc.); see if it might be appropriate to make one of these elements stronger and use it as a repetitive element. Repetition also helps strengthen the reader's sense of recognition of the entity represented by the design.

Your Attitude is Your Life ▾

Lessons from
raising three children
as a single mom

▲

Robin Williams
October 9

The distinctive typeface in the **title** is repeated in the author's **name,** which strengthens their connection even though they are physically far apart on the page. The font for the other text is now in the light weight.

The small triangles were added specifically to create a repetition. Although they point in different directions, the triangular shape is distinct enough to be recognized each time.

The color of the triangles is also a repeated element. Repetition helps tie separate parts of a design together.

Contrast

Would you agree that the example on this page attracts your eye more than the example on the previous page? It's the contrast here, the strong black versus white, that does it. You can add contrast in many ways—rules (lines), typefaces, colors, spatial relationships, directions, etc. The second half of this book discusses the specific topic of contrasting type.

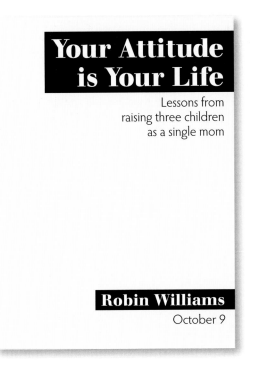

Adding contrast to this was simply a matter of adding the black boxes.

Little Quiz #1: Design principles

Find at least seven differences between the two sample résumés below. Circle each difference and name the design principle it offends. State in words what the changes are.

1 _____

Résumé: Launcelot Gobbo
#73 Acqua Canal
Venice, Italy

Education

- Ravenna Grammar School
- Venice High School, graduated with highest honors
- Trade School for Servants

Work Experience

1593 Kitchen Help, Antipholus Estate
1597 Gardener Apprentice, Tudor Dynasty
1598 Butler Internship, Pembrokes

References

- Shylock the Moneylender
- Bassanio the Golddigger

2 _____

3 _____

4 _____

Résumé
▾ Launcelot Gobbo
#73 Acqua Canal
Venice, Italy

Education
▴ Ravenna Grammar School
▴ Venice High School, graduated
with highest honors
▴ Trade School for Servants

Work Experience
▴ 1593 Kitchen Help, Antipholus Estate
▴ 1597 Gardener Apprentice, Tudor Dynasty
▴ 1598 Butler Internship, Pembrokes

References
▴ Shylock the Moneylender
▴ Bassanio the Golddigger

5 _____

6 _____

7 _____

_____

typefaces
Shannon ExtraBold
Adobe Jenson Pro
ITC Zapf Dingbats ▴

Little Quiz #2: Redesign this ad

What are the problems with this magazine ad? Name the problems so you can find the solutions.

Clues: Is there one main focal point? Why not, and how could you create one? WHY IS SO MUCH OF THE TEXT IN ALL CAPS? Do you need the heavy border *and* the inner boxes? How many different typefaces are in this ad? How many different alignments? Are the logical elements grouped together into close proximity? What could you use as repetitive elements?

Take a piece of tracing paper and trace the outline of the ad. Then move that paper around and trace the individual elements, rearranging them into a more professional, clean, direct advertisement. Work your way through each principle: proximity, alignment, repetition, and contrast. Some suggestions as to where to begin are on the following pages.

THE SHAKESPEARE PAPERS
SHAKESPEARE BY DESIGN

http://www.theshakespearepapers.com

THE SHAKESPEARE PAPERS ARE BIMONTHLY
BOOKLETS OF AMUSING, TANTALIZING,
PECULIAR, EDUCATIVE, UNEXPECTED,
BRILLIANT, SURPRISING, INTRIGUING, AND
OCCASIONALLY CONTROVERSIAL TIDBITS
ABOUT THE SHAKESPEAREAN PLAYS AND
SONNETS.

ONLY $35 A YEAR FOR SIX COLLECTIBLE
ISSUES

SUBSCRIPTION-
BASED

CALL OR EMAIL
cleo@theshakespearepapers.com

7 Sweet Swan Lane
Cygnet City, CALIF. 94536
phone (505) 424-7926

typefaces
Wade Sans Light
Helvetica Neue
Bold Oblique
Trade Gothic Medium
Verdana Regular
Times New Roman
Viceroy

Little Quiz #2 continued: Suggestions for designing an ad
Knowing where to begin can sometimes seem overwhelming. So first
of all, let's clean it up.

First get rid of everything superfluous so you know what you're working
with. For instance, you don't need "http://" (or even "www") in a web
address. You don't need the words "phone," "call," or "email" because
the format of the text and numbers tells you what the item is. You don't
need FOUR logos. You don't need the inner boxes. You don't need all
caps. You don't need CALIF. (it's messy); use CA or spell it out. You don't
need parentheses around the area code.

The rounded edges of the border make this ad look wimpy; it also conflicts
with the sharp edges of the logo. So make the border thinner and sharp
(if your ad is in color, perhaps you could use a pale tint shape instead of
any border at all). Choose one or two typefaces.

The Shakespeare Papers
Shakespeare by Design

TheShakespearePapers.com

The Shakespeare Papers are bimonthly booklets
of amusing, tantalizing, peculiar, educative,
unexpected, brilliant, surprising, intriguing,
and occasionally controversial tidbits about the
Shakespearean plays and sonnets.

Only $38 a year for six collectible issues

subscription-based   call or email
              cleo@TheShakespearePapers.com

7 Sweet Swan Lane
Cygnet City, CA 94536
505.424.7926

Web
and email
addresses
are easier
to read if
you cap
the main
words.

typefaces
Wade Sans Light
Brioso Pro Light
and Bold Italic

Now that you can see what you're really working with, determine what should be the focal point. The focal point might be slightly different depending on where the ad is placed. For instance, if it's a phone book ad for an optometrist, the focal point might be on "Optometry" rather than the physician's name—a reader is scanning the yellow pages looking for someone *in that field,* not that *doctor's name.* In a phone book, the phone number should have more priority than, say, it would in a flyer that was for an event being held on a specific day and time.

What is the purpose of this piece in this particular magazine (or wherever it is)? That will help you determine the hierarchy of the rest of the information. Which items *should* be grouped together into closer proximity?

Use the space below to sketch in a design possibility. You'll find suggestions and one of the many possible layouts on pages 202–203.

Summary

This concludes the design portion of our presentation. You probably want more examples. Examples are all around you—what I most hope to have painlessly instilled in you is an **increased visual awareness.** I thought about providing "cookie cutter" designs, but, as it has been said so truly, it is better to give you a fishing pole than a fish.

Keep in mind that professional designers are always "stealing" other ideas; they are constantly looking around for inspiration. If you're doing a flyer, find a flyer you really like and adapt the layout. Simply by using your own text and graphics, the original flyer turns into your own unique flyer. Find a business card you like and adapt it to your own. Find a newsletter masthead you like and adapt it to your own. *It changes in the adaptation and becomes yours.* We all do it.

If you haven't already, I strongly recommend you read *The Mac is not a typewriter* or *The PC is not a typewriter.* If you are still typing two spaces after periods, if you are underlining text, if you are not using true apostrophes and quotation marks (" and ", not "), then you *seriously* need to read one of those books (or at least skip to *The Non-Designer's Type Book*).

And when you're finished with this book and have absorbed all of the concepts, check out *Robin Williams Design Workshop.* It explains and displays more advanced design concepts.

For now, have fun. Lighten up. Don't take all this design stuff too seriously. I guarantee that if you simply follow Robin's Four Principles of Design, you will be creating dynamic, interesting, organized pages you will be proud of.

Using Color

This is a wonderful time in the world of graphic design. Everyone now has color printers on their desktops, and professional color printing has never in the history of this planet been so available and affordable. (Search the web for color printing and compare prices.)

Color theory can get very complex, but in this chapter I'm just going to provide a brief explanation of the color wheel and how to use it. A color wheel is amazingly useful when you need to make a conscious decision about choosing colors for a project.

And I'll briefly explain the difference between the color models CMYK and RGB and when to use each one.

As you can see in this simple example, color not only has its own impact, but it impacts all objects around it.

The amazing color wheel

The color wheel begins with yellow, red, and blue. These are called the **primary colors** because they're the only colors you can't create. That is, if you have a box of watercolors, you know you can mix blue and yellow to make green, but there is no way to mix pure yellow, red, or blue from other colors.

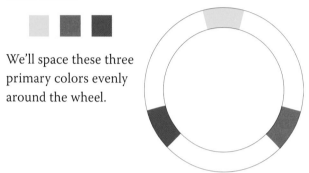

We'll space these three primary colors evenly around the wheel.

Now, if you take your watercolor box and mix each of these colors with an equal amount of the one next to it, you'll get the **secondary colors.** As you're probably aware from working with crayons and watercolors as a kid, yellow and blue make green; blue and red make purple; red and yellow make orange.

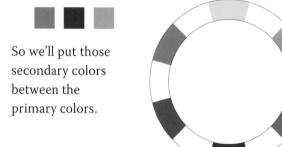

So we'll put those secondary colors between the primary colors.

To fill in the empty spots in the color wheel, you probably know what to do—mix equal parts of the colors on each side. These are called the **tertiary** (or third) **colors.** That is, yellow and orange make, well, yellow-orange. And blue and green make blue-green (which I'll call aqua).

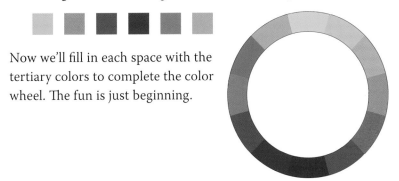

Now we'll fill in each space with the tertiary colors to complete the color wheel. The fun is just beginning.

Color relationships

So now we have a color wheel with the basic twelve colors. With this color wheel, we can create combinations of colors that are pretty much guaranteed to work together. On the following pages, we'll explore the various ways to do this.

(In the CMYK color model we're using, as explained on page 106, the "color" black is actually the combination of all colors, and the "color" white is an absence of all colors.)

Complementary

Colors directly across from each other, exact opposites, are **complements.**
Because they're so opposite, they often work best when one is the main
color and the other is an accent.

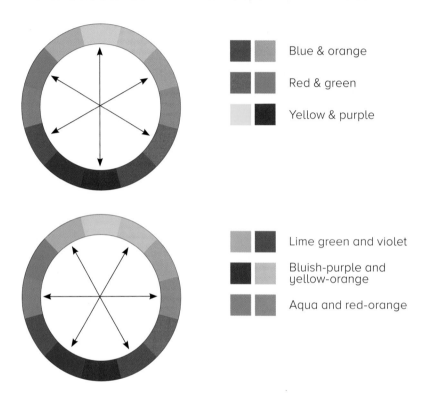

Blue & orange

Red & green

Yellow & purple

Lime green and violet

Bluish-purple and yellow-orange

Aqua and red-orange

Now, you might think some of the color combinations on
these pages are pretty weird. But that's the great thing about
knowing how to use the color wheel—you can gleefully use
these weird combinations and know that you have permission
to do so! They really do work well together.

typefaces
Tabitha
Snell Roundhand Bold

Triads

A set of three colors equidistant from each other always creates a **triad** of pleasing colors. Red, yellow, and blue is an extremely popular combination for children's products. Because these are the primary colors, this combination is called the **primary triad.**

Experiment with the **secondary triad** of green, orange, and purple—not as common, but an exciting combination for that very reason.

All triads (except the primary triad of red, yellow, and blue) have underlying colors connecting them, which makes them harmonize well.

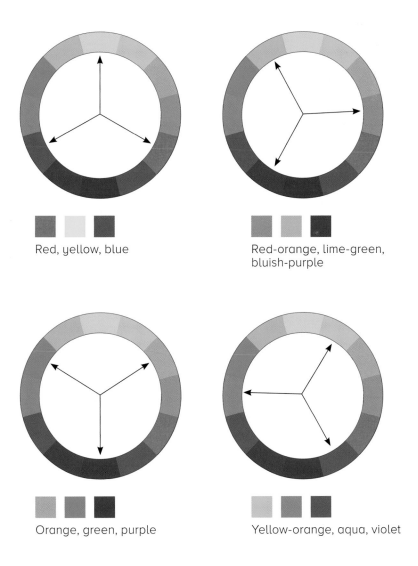

Red, yellow, blue

Red-orange, lime-green, bluish-purple

Orange, green, purple

Yellow-orange, aqua, violet

Split complement triads

Another form of a triad is the **split complement.** Choose a color from one side of the wheel, find its complement directly across the wheel, but use the colors *on each side of the complement* instead of the complement itself. This creates a combination that has a little more sophisticated edge to it. Below are just a couple of the various combinations.

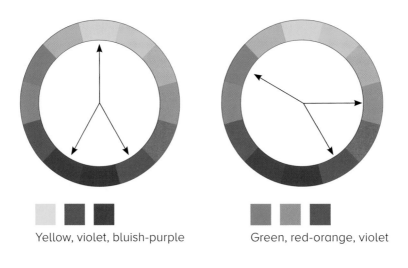

Yellow, violet, bluish-purple

Green, red-orange, violet

I used a tint of the color in "Tricksy Words" for the box behind the text. See pages 98–101 for information about tints.

typefaces
Wendy Bold
Myriad Pro Condensed

Analogous colors

An **analogous** combination is composed of those colors that are next to each other on the wheel. No matter which two or three you combine, they all share an undertone of the same color, creating a harmonious combination. Combine an analogous group of colors with their various tints and shades, as explained on the following page, and you've got lots to work with!

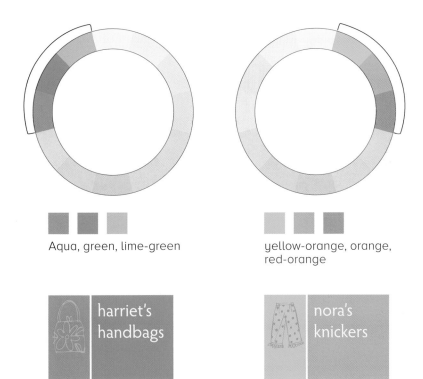

Aqua, green, lime-green

yellow-orange, orange, red-orange

harriet's handbags

nora's knickers

typefaces
Hypatia Sans Pro Regular
Diva Doodles

Shades and tints

The basic color wheel that we've been working with so far involves only the pure "hue," or the pure color. We can hugely expand the wheel and thus our options simply by adding black or white to the various hues.

The pure color is the **hue.**

Add black to a hue to create a **shade.**

Add white to a hue to create a **tint.**

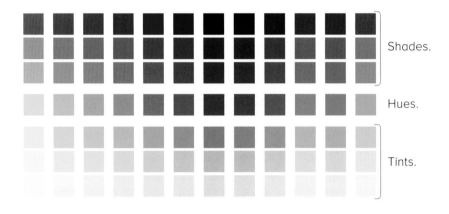

Shades.

Hues.

Tints.

Below is what the colors look like in the wheel. What you see here are colored bands, but it's really a continuous gradient with an infinite number of colors from white to black.

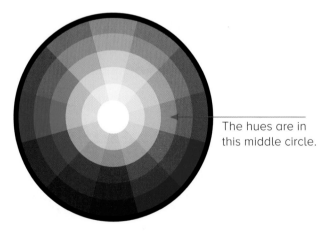

The hues are in this middle circle.

Make your own shades and tints

If your software program allows you to create your own colors, just add black to a color to create a shade. To make a tint, use the tint slider your application provides. Check your software manual.

If your application provides a color palette something like this one, here's how to make tints and shades.

First, make sure to select the color wheel icon in the toolbar (circled).

Make sure the slider is at the top of the colored bar on the right.

The tiny dot inside the color wheel selects the color.

Hues are on the outer rim of this particular wheel.

To create a tint, drag the tiny dot toward the center of the wheel.

The color bar at the top displays the color you've selected.

To save that exact color for use again, press on that upper color bar and drag—it will create a tiny color box. Drop that color box into one of the empty slots at the bottom.

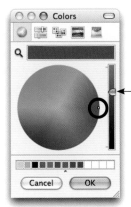

To create a shade, position the tiny dot on the color of which you want to make a shade.

Drag the slider on the right downward. You'll get millions of subtle options.

To save that exact color for use again, see above.

Monochromatic colors

A **monochromatic** combination is composed of one hue with any number of its corresponding tints and shades.

You're actually very familiar with a monochromatic scheme—any black and white photograph is made of black (the "hue," although black isn't really a "color") and many tints, or varying shades of gray. You know how beautifully that can work. So have fun with a design project using a monochromatic combination.

This is the orange hue with several of its shades and tints. You can actually reproduce the effect of a number of colors in a one-color print job; use shades and tints of black, then have it printed with the ink color of your choice.

Orange.

This postcard is set up using only tints of black.

This is the same job as above, but printed using dark brown ink instead of black. The tints of black become tints of the ink color.

typefaces
Stoclet Light **and Bold**
Renfield's Lunch
Gargoonies

Shades and tints in combination

Most fun of all, choose one of the four color relationships described on pages 93–97, but instead of using the hues, use various tints and shades of those colors. This expands your options tremendously, but you can still feel safe that the colors "work" together.

For instance, the combination of red and green is a perfect complement, but it's almost impossible to get away from a Christmas effect. However, if you dip into the *shades* of these complementary colors, riches appear.

I mentioned that the combination of the primary colors of blue, red, and yellow is extremely popular for children's products. So popular, in fact, that it's difficult to get away from the kids' look. Unless you bring in some of the tints and shades—voilà! Rich and delicious combinations.

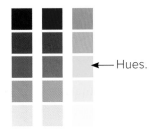

←—Hues.

typefaces

Scriptease

Proxima Nova Alt ExtraBold

fRaNces uNciaL

Hypatia Sans Pro Regular

Watch the tones

Are there any colors that don't look great together? Not if you subscribe to Robin's Wildflower Theory of Color—have you ever seen a field of wildflowers and said, "Omigosh, that's a dreadful combination of colors in that field." Probably not.

But what that field of wildflowers automatically includes is a variety of **tones,** of different values of colors. About the only thing that is guaranteed to cause visual twitching because of color combinations is if the tones are too similar.

Tone refers to the particular quality of brightness, deepness, or hue of any color. As you can see in the first examples below, when the tones are similar, it gets a little muddy looking. The contrast is too weak. If you were to reproduce the examples below on a copy machine, the text would get lost.

If your design calls for hues with similar tones, try not to bump them up together, and don't use the same amounts of each one.

The tones of these dark colors are much too close, as you can obviously see.

The contrast is much better here; the contrast is a result of differences in tones. Where there might be some trouble (in the white ornament on the pale tint), I added a bit of a shadow to separate the two elements. I did the same on the previous page where the red text was having a hard time on the blue field—their values are too close.

Warm colors vs. cool colors

Colors tend to be either on the warm side (which means they have some red or yellow in them) or on the cool side (which means they have some blue in them). You can "warm up" certain colors, such as grays or tans, by adding more reds or yellows to them. Conversely, you can cool down some colors by adding various blues to them.

But the more practical thing that I want you to remember is that cool colors recede into the background, and warm colors come to the front. It takes very little of a hot color to make an impact—reds and yellow jump right into your eyes. So if you're combining hot colors with cool, always use less of the hot color.

Cool colors recede, so you can use (sometimes you *have* to use) more of a cool color to make an impact or to contrast effectively.

Don't try to even it out! Take advantage of this visual phenomenon.

Sunrise on the Nile
Music from the waters of life by
Umm Kulthum

An excess of red is overwhelming and rather annoying.

Sunrise on the Nile
Music from the waters of life by
Umm Kulthum

Here we picked up the red from the bucket in the photo to use as an accent.

typeface
Tapioca

How to begin to choose?

Sometimes it can seem overwhelming to choose colors. Start with a logical approach. Is it a seasonal project you're working on? Perhaps use analogous colors (page 97) that connote the seasons—hot reds and yellows for summer; cool blues for winter; shades of oranges & browns for autumn; bright greens for spring.

Are there official company colors to work with? Perhaps you can start there and use tints and shades. Are you working with a logo that has specific colors in it? Perhaps use a split complement of its colors (page 96).

Does your project include a photograph or other image? Pick up a color in the photograph and choose a range of other colors based on that. You might want analogous colors to keep the project sedate and calm, or complementary colors to add some visual excitement.

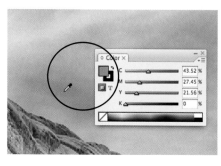

Here I picked up the color of the sky to use for the main title. For the rest of the project, I might use the colors analogous to the sandy color of the cliffs, with that blue tint for accents.

In some applications, you might have an eyedropper tool with which you can pick up colors you click on. That's how I got the color of the sky and of the cliffs in InDesign.

typefaces
ITC Arid
Proxima Nova Alt Light

If you're working on a project that recurs regularly, you might want to make yourself a color palette that you'll consistently refer to for all projects.

For instance, I publish a sixteen-page booklet every two months on some tidbit of the Shakespearean works. There are six main themes that recur every year, so after collecting them for a few years, the color-coding becomes an organizational tool. I chose 80-percent tints of the six tertiary colors (page 93) for the main color blocks on the covers; the color wraps around a bit and the title is always reversed out. This choice provides me with a color structure for the interiors.

If you're beginning a new project that's composed of a number of different pieces, try choosing your color palette before you begin. It will make a lot of decisions easier for you along the way.

typefaces
Wade Sans Light

CMYK vs. RGB; print vs. web

There are two important color models to be aware of. Here is the briefest of explanations on a very complex topic. If all you ever do is print to your little desktop color inkjet, you can get by without knowing anything about color models, so you can skip this for now. It will be here when you need it.

CMYK

CMYK stands for Cyan (which is a blue), Magenta (which is sort of red/pink), Yellow, and a Key color, which is usually black. With these four colors of ink, we can print many thousands of colors, which is why it's called a "four-color process." (Specialized print jobs can include extra colors of inks.)

The colors in CMYK are like our coloring crayons or paint boxes—blue and yellow make green, etc. This is the model we've been using throughout this chapter because this is a printed book.

CMYK is the color model you'll use for projects that are going to be printed by a printing press onto something physical. Just about everything you ever see printed in a book, a magazine, a poster, on matchbox covers or cookie boxes has been printed with CMYK.

Take a look at a printed color image with a magnifying glass and you'll be able to see the "rosettes" made up of the dots of color.

RGB

RGB stands for Red, Green, and Blue. RGB is what you see on your computer monitor, television, iPhone, etc.

In RGB, if you mix red and green you get—yellow. Really. Mix full-strength blue and red and you get hot pink. That's because rgb is composed of beams of colored light that are not reflected off of any physical object—it is light that goes straight from the monitor into your eyes. If you mix all the colors together you get white, and if you delete all the colors, you get black.

In the world, the spectrum of visible light hits objects. Objects absorb (or subtract) most of the spectrum—what they don't absorb reflects back to our eyes as color.

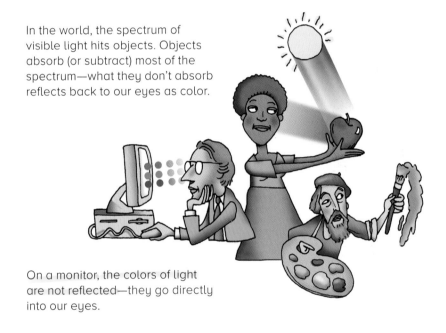

On a monitor, the colors of light are not reflected—they go directly into our eyes.

Print vs. web color models

The important thing to remember about CMYK and RGB is this:

> **Use CMYK for projects that are to be printed.**
> **Use RGB for anything that will be viewed on a screen.**

If you're printing to an expensive digital color printer (instead of a four-color printing press), check with the press operator to see whether they want all colors in CMYK or RGB.

RGB makes smaller file sizes, and some techniques in Photoshop work only (or best and usually faster) in RGB. But switching back and forth from CMYK to RGB loses a little data each time, so it's best to work on your images in RGB and change them to CMYK as the last thing you do.

Because RGB works through light that goes straight into our eyes, the images on the screen are gorgeous and backlit with an astonishing range of colors. Unfortunately, when you switch to CMYK and then print that with ink on paper, you lose some of that brilliance and range. That's just what happens, so don't be too disappointed.

Extra Tips & Tricks

In this chapter we'll look at creating a variety of advertising and promotional pieces for a fictional company called Url's Internet Cafe.* I add lots of other tips and tricks and techniques in this section, but you'll see where the four basic principles apply to every project, no matter how big or small.

This section includes specific tips for designing your business cards, letterhead, envelopes, flyers, newsletters, brochures, direct-mail postcards, newspaper ads, and web sites.

* There really is an UrlsInternetCafe.com, but the products you see in this chapter are not for sale. Well, they *were* for sale, but the online fulfillment company we used went out of business and our great products disappeared. If you see them anywhere, please let us know.

Creating a package

One of the most important features of an identity package follows the principle of repetition: there must be some identifying image or style that carries throughout every piece. Take a look at the individual pieces below, all for the Cafe. Name the repetitive elements.

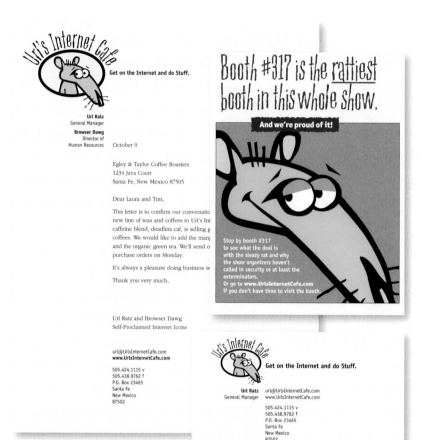

Business cards

If you use a second color, consider using it sparingly. Most of the time a tiny bit is more effective than throwing the second color all over the card. You get your money's worth with just a splash.

Talk to the print shop about how many copies of the card to set up on one page, and how far apart. Ask if you can send them an Adobe Acrobat PDF file to print from (if you don't know how to make a PDF, you'll find details on Adobe's web site, www.Adobe.com). Or buy those perforated, preprinted business cards that you can run through your own office printer.

Business card size

Standard business card size in the U.S. is 3.5 inches wide by 2 inches tall (8.5cm x 5.5cm in many other countries). A vertical format, of course, would be 2 inches wide by 3.5 inches tall.

Url's Internet Cafe

Url Ratz, Manager
505·424·1115

url@UrlsInternetCafe.com
www.UrlsInternetCafe.com
P.O. Box 23465 • Santa Fe • New Mexico 87502

typefaces
Pious Henry
Officina Sans Book **and Bold**

Tips on designing business cards

Business cards can be a challenge to design because you usually need to pack a lot of information into a small space. And the amount of information you put on a business card has been growing—in addition to the standard address and phone, now you probably need your cell number, fax number, email address, and if you have a web site (which you should), your web address.

Format

Your first choice is whether to work with a **horizontal** format or a **vertical one.** Just because most cards are horizontal doesn't mean they *have* to be. Very often the information fits better in a vertical layout, especially when we have so many pieces of information to include on such a little card. Experiment with both vertical and horizontal layouts, *and choose the one that works best for the information you have on your card.*

Type size

One of the biggest problems with business cards designed by new designers is the type size. It's usually **too big.** Even the 10- or 11-point type we read in books looks horsey on a small card. And 12-point type looks downright dorky. I know it's difficult at first to use 9- or even 8- or 7-point type, but look at the business cards you've collected. Pick out three that look the most professional and sophisticated. They don't use 12-point type.

Keep in mind that a business card is not a book, a brochure, or even an ad—a business card contains information that a client only needs to look at for a couple of seconds. Sometimes the overall, sophisticated effect of the card's design is actually more important than making the type big enough for your great-grandmother to read easily.

Create a consistent image on all pieces

If you plan to create a letterhead and matching envelopes, you really need to design all three pieces at once. The entire package of business cards, letterhead, and envelopes should present a **consistent image** to clients and customers.

Letterhead and envelopes

Few people look at a company's stationery and think, "This is so beautiful, I'll triple my order," or "This is so ugly, I'll cancel my order." But when people see your stationery, they think *something* about you and it's going to be positive or negative, depending on the design and feel of that stationery.

From the quality of the paper you choose to the design, color, typeface, and the envelope, the implied message should inspire confidence in your business. The content of your letter, of course, will carry substantial weight, but don't overlook the unconscious influence exerted by the letterhead itself.

Be brave! Be bold!

Url Ratz
General Manager

Browser Dawg
Director of
Human Resources

url@UrlsInternetCafe.com
www.UrlsInternetCafe.com

505.424.1115 v • 505.438.9762 f
P.O. Box 23465 • Santa Fe • New Mexico • 87502

Don't do this!

P.O. Box 23465, Santa Fe, NM, 87502
(505) 424-1115 telephone (505) 438-9762 fax

October 9

Egley and Taylor Coffee Roasters
1234 Java Court
Santa Fe, New Mexico 87505

Dear Laura and Tim,

This letter is to confirm our conversation regarding adding a new line of teas and coffees to
Url's Internet Cafe. The high-caffeine blend, deadline.caf, is selling great, as are the other
coffees. We would like to add the mango-pekoe blend tea and the organic green tea. We'll
send over the contract and purchase orders on Monday.

It's always a pleasure doing business with you!

Thank you very much,

Url Ratz and Browser Dawg
Self-Proclaimed Internet Icons

Don't use
a different
arrangement on
the envelope
from what you
use on the
letterhead and
the business
card! All three
items should
look like they
belong together.

Url Ratz   General Manager

Url's Internet Cafe
Get on the Internet and do Stuff.

e-mail: (505) 424-1115 ph.
url@UrlsInternetCafe.com   P.O. Box 23465
www.UrlsInternetCafe.com   Santa Fe, NM 87502

Url's Internet Cafe
P.O. Box 23465
Santa Fe, NM 87502

Don't center everything on the page, unless your logo is an
obviously centered logo and you must work with it. If you do
center, try to be a little more creative with the type, the size,
or the placement of the items (that is, even though the items
are centered with each other, perhaps they don't have to be
directly centered on the page; try placing the entire centered
arrangement closer to the left side).

Don't use Times, Arial, Helvetica, or Sand.

Just as on your business card, avoid parentheses, abbreviations,
and superfluous words that just add clutter.

Try this . . .

Notice how these three pieces have essentially the same layout. Work on all three pieces at the same time to make sure your chosen layout will work in each situation.

October 9

Egley & Taylor Coffee Roasters
1234 Java Court
Santa Fe, New Mexico 87505

Dear Laura and Tim,

This letter is to confirm our conversation regarding adding a new line of teas and coffees to Url's Internet Cafe. The high-caffeine blend, deadline.caf, is selling great, as are the other coffees. We would like to add the mango-pekoe blend tea and the organic green tea. We'll send over the contract and purchase orders on Monday.

It's always a pleasure doing business with you!

Thank you very much,

Url Ratz and Browser Dawg
Self-Proclaimed Internet Icons

url@UrlsInternetCafe.com
www.UrlsInternetCafe.com

505.424.1115 v
505.438.9762 f
P.O. Box 23465
Santa Fe
New Mexico
87502

Feel free to use type and graphics in a huge way or a small way.

Uncenter the format. Those strong lines of flush left and flush right add strength to your design.

Tips on letterhead and envelope design

Design your letterhead and envelope at the same time as your business card. They should look like they belong together—if you give someone a business card and then later send a letter, those pieces should reinforce each other.

Envelope size

The standard business envelope is **9½ x 4⅛ inches.** It's called a #10 envelope. The European size is 110 mm x 220 mm, and it's called a C4 envelope.

Create a focal point

One element should be **dominant,** and it should be dominant in the same way on the letterhead, the envelope, and the business card. Please avoid the boring centered-across-the-top layout on the letterhead!

Alignment

Choose one **alignment** for your stationery! Don't center something across the top and then put the rest of the text flush left. Be brave—try flush right down the side with lots of linespacing. Try setting your company name in huge letters across the top. Try placing your logo (or a piece of it) huge and light as a shadow beneath the area where you will type.

On the letterhead, make sure to arrange the elements so when you type the actual letter, the text fits neatly into the design of the stationery.

Second page

If you can afford to make a second page to your stationary, take a **small element** that appears on your first page and use it all by itself on a second page. If you are planning to print, say, 1,000 sheets of letterhead, you can usually ask the printshop to print something like 800 of the first page and 200 of the second page. Even if you don't plan to print a second page, ask the printer for several hundred blank sheets of the same paper so you have *something* on which to write longer letters.

Faxing and copying

If you ever plan to send your letterhead through **fax** or **copy machines,** don't choose a dark paper or one that has lots of speckles in it. Also avoid large areas of dark ink, reverse type, or tiny type that will get lost in the process. If you do a *lot* of faxing, you might want to create two versions of your letterhead—one for print and one for fax.

Flyers

Flyers are great fun to create because you can safely abandon restraint! This is a great place to go wild and really call attention to yourself. As you know, flyers compete with all the other readable junk in the world, especially with other flyers. Often they are posted on a bulletin board with dozens of competing pages that are all trying to grab the attention of passers-by.

A flyer is one of the best places to use fun and different typefaces, and a fun face is one of the best ways to **call attention** to a headline. Don't be a wimp—this is your chance to use one of those really off-the-wall faces you've been lusting after!

And what a great place to experiment with graphics. Just try making the graphic image or photograph at least twice the size you originally planned. Or make the headline 400 point instead of 24. Or create a minimalist flyer with one line of 10-point type in the middle of the page and a small block of text at the bottom. Anything out of the ordinary will make people stop and look, and that is 90 percent of your goal.

Url's own java,
deadline.caf,
now available

Url's Internet Cafe
High-caffeine brew to keep you working all through the night.

Don't do this!

*Booth #317 is the rattiest booth in this whole show.
And we're proud of it.*

Stop by booth #317 to see what the deal is with the sleazy rat and why the show organizers haven't called in security or at least the exterminators.

Or go to www.UrlsInternet-Cafe.com if you don't have time to visit the booth.

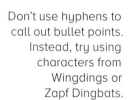

Don't put everything in boxes! Let the strong alignment create the "box" around the text.

As in everything else, don't set the same amount of space between all elements. If items are part of a unit, group them closer together.

Don't use Times, Arial, Helvetica, or Sand.

ATTENTION CONFERENCE AT-TENDEES:

- Never before has this conference allowed booth space for such a disgusting character as Url Ratz.

- Stop by booth #317 to see what possible redeeming traits he could possibly have that would allow someone like him into this ex-hibit hall.

-While you're there, get some free stuff be-fore they call in the exterminators.

- Or stop by his web site: www.UrlsInternet-Cafe.com

URL'S INTERNET CAFE
www.UrlsInternetCafe.com

Don't use hyphens to call out bullet points. Instead, try using characters from Wingdings or Zapf Dingbats.

Don't center everything on the page and then put small pieces of text in the corners!

Avoid a gray, boring page—add contrast.

Watch the line endings—there's no need to break lines at awkward places or to hyphenate unnecessarily.

Try this . . .

Booth #317 is the ratttest booth in this whole show.

And we're proud of it!

Stop by booth #317 to see what the deal is with the sleazy rat and why the show organizers haven't called in security or at least the exterminators.
Or go to www.UrlsInternetC if you don't have time to visit

Use a huge headline or huge clip art.

Use an interesting typeface in a huge way.

Crop a photograph or clip art into a tall narrow shape; place it along the left edge; align the text flush left.

Or place the art along the right edge and align the text flush right.

Or set the text in several columns, each one flush left.

It's okay to set the body text small on a flyer. If you capture the reader's attention in the first place, she will read the small type.

Attention Conference Attendees:

Never before has this conference allowed booth space for such a disgusting character as Url Ratz. Visit booth #317 and ask about possible redeeming traits that might allow someone like him into this respectable exhibit hall. While you're there, get some of the free stuff stamped with **www.UrlsInternetCafe.com** before someone calls an exterminator.

There's a Rat in Booth #317

Tips on designing flyers

The biggest problems with most flyers created by new designers are a lack of contrast and a presentation of information that has no hierarchy. That is, the initial tendency is to make everything large, thinking that it needs to grab someone's attention. But if *everything* is large, then *nothing* can really grab a reader's attention. Use a strong focal point and contrast to organize the information and lead the reader's eye through the page.

Create a focal point

Put one thing on your page that is huge and interesting and **strong.** If you catch their eye with your focal point, they are more likely to read the rest of the text.

Use subheads that contrast

After the focal point, use strong subheads (strong visually, and strong in what it says) so readers can quickly **scan** the flyer to determine the point of the message. If the subheads don't interest them, they're not going to read the copy. But if there are no subheads at all and readers have to read every word on the flyer to understand what it's about, they're going to toss it rather than spend the time deciphering the text.

Repetition

Whether your headline uses an ugly typeface, a beautiful one, or an ordinary one in an unusual way, try to pull a little of that same font into the body of the text for **repetition.** Perhaps use just one letter or one word in that same typeface. Use it as your subheads, initial caps, or perhaps as bullets. A strong contrast of typefaces will add interest to your flyer.

Alignment

And remember, choose one alignment! Don't center the headline and then set the body copy flush left, or don't center everything on the page and then stick things in the corners at the bottom. Be strong. Be brave. Try all flush left or flush right.

Newsletters

One of the most important features of a multiple-page publication is consistency, or **repetition.** Every page should look like it belongs to the whole piece. You can do this with color, graphic style, fonts, spatial arrangements, bulleted lists that repeat a formatting style, borders around photographs, captions, etc.

Now, this doesn't mean that everything has to look exactly the same! But (just as in life) if you have a solid foundation you can get away with breaking out of that foundation with glee (and people won't worry about you). Experiment with graphics at a tilt or photographs cropped very wide and narrow and spread across three columns. With that solid foundation, you can set something like the president's letter for your newsletter in a special format and it will really stand out.

It's okay to have white space (empty space) in your newsletter. But don't let the white space become "trapped" between other elements. The white space needs to be as organized as the visible elements. Let it be there, and let it flow.

One of the first and most fun things to design in a newsletter is the flag (sometimes called the masthead, although the masthead is actually the part inside that tells you who runs the magazine). The flag is the piece that sets the tone for the rest of the newsletter.

Don't do this!

RAT TALES
News from Url's Internet Cafe
Volume 1, Number 1

What's Up at Url's Internet Cafe?

There's always somethin' happening at Url's Internet Cafe. Drop in anytime, day or night—we're open twenty-four/seven. You'll always find friends, enemies, ratz, coffee, t-shirts you just gotta have, advice, cartoons, witty sports insights, surprises, provocative conversation if you're really lucky, and a few laughs.

FOR BEGINNERS ONLY

If you're new to Internet and this World Wide Web, stop at the front porch and have Browser NetHound give You'll fascin to trav to find very fi cuddl

THI Fro can o blend octan

guaranteed to keep you awake and working all night.

THE SPORTS BAR
Get an Url's-eye view of what's happening in the sports world. You won't hear this on prime time!

THE NAVIGATION BAR
Coming soon! Even we don't know what this is yet!

THE GIFT SHOP AND BOOKSTORE
Be the first in your studio (maybe the first in the world!)

show is totally integrated with the web site to the point where you, the viewer, can tell the producers what you think, what you want to see more or less of, whom you want to see as guests, and more. Details on the web site!

THE CHANGING ROOM
Meet dear Amanda Reckonwith, the most stunning and witty drag queen on the Internet. "Change your mind, change your future, but at least change your wardrobe!"

THE BACK PORCH
Come on out to the back porch

Don't be a wimp about your flag (the title of your newsletter on the front page). Tell people who you are!

Don't create a flat, gray newsletter. Use contrasting type where appropriate, create pull-quotes, and add other visually interesting elements to pull the reader's eye into the page.

You want products? We got products!

Would you buy a lab coat from an ugly rat? You might not think so now, but just wait 'til you see the lab coats, t-shirts, caps, polo shirts, special coffees, teas, mugs, RatPadz, and other great gift ideas at Url's Internet Cafe.

You need a lab coat. You could also use a t-shirt that tells your clients the Internet facts of life. And coffees blended specifically for web surfers. You'll need matching mugs for the coffee and most likely you'll want original RatPadz to replace those clunky old mouse pads you have just lying around the office.

Did we mention polo shirts, caps, gift boxes, and do-rags? Prepare yourself for the Technology Age: t-shirt gift ideas and a cafe full of education, fun stuff and a lot of loonies.

Are you really reading this tiny little type? You might not think so now, but just wait 'til you see the lab coats, t-shirts, caps, polo shirts, special coffees, teas, mugs, RatPadz, and other great gift ideas at Url's Internet Cafe.

You need a lab coat. You could also use a t-shirt that tells your clients the Internet facts of life. And coffees blended specifically for web surfers. You'll need match most i RatPa

old mouse pads you have just lying around the office.

Did we mention polo shirts, caps, gift boxes, and do-rags? Still reading? Did you notice this is just really boring text that's repeated over and over again? Why on earth are you wasting your time? Get back to work!

Would you buy a lab coat from an ugly rat? You might not think so now, but just wait 'til you see the lab coats, t-shirts, caps, polo shirts, special coffees, teas, mugs, RatPadz, and other great gift ideas at Url's Internet Cafe.

You need a lab coat. You could also use a t-shirt that tells your clients the Internet facts of life. And Robin adores John. You'll need matching mugs for the coffee and most likely you'll want original RatPadz to replace those clunky old mouse pads you have just lying around the office.

Did we mention that you can quit reading this now? Prepare

And for beginners only

If you've never been to the World Wide Web before, or if you're still a little new and intimidated, let Browser show you around. Walk through this web site and learn the difference between the Internet and the World Wide Web; what exactly are web pages; what's a browser and why do you need one; what are search engines, where do you find them, and how do you use them to find specific items of interest; how to get around web pages; what to expect from the Internet; how to "download" files; how to customize your browser so it suits the way you want to surf; and even how to make your own web page.

There's also a glossary of common Internet-related terms with definitions you can actually understand, and sources for where you can find more information about all sorts of aspects of the Internet and the World Wide Web. By the time you finish touring Browser's beginner site, you won't be a beginner anymore!

THE SITCOM!

Url's Internet Cafe is a television sitcom, a cross between "Cheers" and "Seinfeld," that takes place in Url's Internet Cafe. Url's Cafe is an old clapboard house with a front porch, back porch, basement, and attic. Inside, Url's is a comfortable, interesting place that doesn't look very high-tech, except that it has lots of computers connected to a high-speed line. This hilarious sitcom provides computer nerds with a light-hearted look at this Internet world we're living in, and gives non-computer people a peek into that online world in a different way. It ties in all those things that even the general public has an inkling of—computer relationships, addicts, seniors online, etc.

There are, of course, the stars of the show and the standard stereotypes who appear regularly. But the show also features regular guest appearances by people like Guy Kawasaki, Bob LeVitus, Steve Wozniak, the Netscape boys, the Yahoo boys, and Kai Krause, as well as football, basketball, and boxing stars who have home pages. And Letterman, the other d Williams, Hillary Clinton,

Scott Adams, and Dave Barry all stop by now and then because they're technogeeks.

The Cast of Characters

Url Ratz, proprietor of the cafe. He's sleazy but lovable rat. "On the Internet, I'm rich and I'm handsome and I sing well, too." He loves this technology, but is also a little disdainful of it.

Browser Dawg, the dog (on the sitcom, he's a real dog.) On the web site, Browser is the one who teaches beginners about the Internet and the World Wide Web. He loves everything and everybody. Except DimmSimm and her son-in-law.

Amanda Reckonwith, drag queen, hangs out in the basement. "Come down to my level," she says. Amanda writes a hilarious spoof advice column on the web site.

Grandma Ada, the tech support. She's a bit crabby, but is incredibly smart about technology. Puts the young punks in their places regularly. Flirts with old men. Has several online sweethearts.

Pixel, Url's girlfriend, is a cranky neo-Luddite. She smudges with burning sage, brings in tarot card readers and palm readers and drummers and

digeridoo players, sprays users with aroma-therapy waters, etc. She has also arranged for Url's Internet Cafe to be the Alien Headquarters, much to Url's chagrin, as well as the place with the most frequent Elvis sightings.

DimmSimm, the landlady. She is mean and unappreciative, no matter what people do for her. Her favorite phrase is "I sue you!" When confronted, she pretends not to speak English.

Gig Megaflop, a has-been actor who drops in occasionally and slanders people he doesn't even know. When confronted, he caustically retorts, "Do you know who I am?" Nobody ever does.

VISIT URL'S INTERNET CAFE TODAY!

There's only one place in the world where you can get such ratty stuff, and that's at our web site. Created by web designers for web designers, we [almost] guarantee you'll find something that makes you happy. Or something that at least makes you smile. And how many rats can make that kind of guarantee? See for yourself at www.**UrlsInternetCafe.com**

Whatever you do, don't write a bunch of filler copy just to fill the space with text. Who wants to read useless words? We have enough to do in our lives. Instead, use that space to be creative! Or just let *there be white space.*

P.O. Box 23465
Santa Fe, New Mexico 87502
505.424.1115 v
505.438.9762

url@UrlsInternetCafe.com
www.UrlsInternetCafe.com

Henrik Birkvig
c/o Den Grafiske Højskole
67 Glentevej
DK-2400 København NV
Denmark

Bulk Rate
Postage
Permit No.
2345

On the other hand, don't use a different typeface and arrangement for every article. If you create a strong, consistent, under-lying structure throughout the newsletter, then you can call attention to a special article by treating it differently.

If everything is different, nothing is special.

Try this . . .

Most people skim through newsletter pages picking out headlines—so make the headlines clear and bold.

You can see the underlying structure of the text here. With the solidity of that structure, the graphics can really juice up the pages by being tilted, enlarged, text-wrapped, etc.

Take a few minutes to verbalize how all four of the basic principles of design appear in a multiple-page publication like this, and notice the effect of each principle.

Tips on designing newsletters

The biggest problems with newsletters seem to be lack of alignment, lack of contrast, and too much Helvetica (Arial is another name for Helvetica).

Alignment

Choose an alignment and stick to it. Trust me—you'll have a stronger and more professional look to your entire newsletter if you maintain that strong edge along the left. And keep everything else aligned. If you use rules (lines), they should begin and end in alignment with something else, like the column edge or column bottom. If your photograph hangs outside the column one-quarter inch, crop it so it aligns instead.

You see, if all the elements are neatly aligned, then when appropriate you can freely break out of that alignment with gusto. But don't be a wimp about breaking the alignment—either align the item or don't. Placement that is a *little bit* out of alignment looks like a mistake. If your photo does not fit neatly into the column, then let it break out of the column boldly, not barely.

Paragraph indents

First paragraphs, even after subheads, should not be indented. When you do indent, use the standard typographic indent of one "em" space, which is a space as wide as the point size of your type; that is, if you're using 11-point type, your indent should be 11 points (about two spaces, not five). Use *either* extra space between paragraphs *or* an indent, but *not* both.

Not Helvetica!

If your newsletter looks a little gray and drab, you can instantly juice it up simply by using a strong, heavy, sans serif typeface for your headlines and subheads. Not Helvetica. The Helvetica or Arial that came with your computer isn't bold enough to create a strong contrast. Invest in a sans serif family that includes a heavy black version as well as a light version (such as Eurostile, Formata, Syntax, Frutiger, or Myriad). Use that heavy black for your headlines and pull-quotes and you'll be amazed at the difference. Or use an appropriate decorative face for the headlines, perhaps in another color.

Readable body copy

For best readability, try a classic oldstyle serif face (such as Garamond, Jenson, Caslon, Minion, or Palatino), or a lightweight slab serif (such as Clarendon, Bookman, Kepler, or New Century Schoolbook). What you're reading right now is Warnock Pro Light from Adobe. If you use a sans serif font, give a little extra linespace (leading) and shorter line lengths.

Brochures

Brochures are a quick and inexpensive way to get the word out about your brand new homemade-pie business, school fundraiser, or upcoming scavenger hunt. Dynamic, well-designed brochures can be "eye candy" for readers, drawing them in and educating them in a delightful and painless way.

Armed with the basic design principles, you can create eye-grabbing brochures of your own. The tips on the next couple of pages will help.

Before you sit down to design the brochure, fold a piece of paper into the intended shape and make notes on each flap. Pretend you just found it—in what order do you read the panels?

Keep in mind the order in which the panels of a brochure are presented to the reader as they open it. For instance, when a reader opens the front cover, they should not be confronted with the copyright and contact information.

The fold measurements are not the same on the front as they are on the back! After you fold your paper sample, measure from left to right on front and back. **Do not simply divide 11 inches into thirds**—it won't work because one panel must be slightly shorter to tuck inside the other panel.

A brochure can be your number-one marketing tool.

It's important to be aware of the folds; you don't want important information disappearing into the creases! **If you have a strong alignment for the text** on each panel of the brochure, however, feel free to let the graphics cross over the space between the columns of text (the **gutter**) and into the fold. See the example on page 129.

The three-fold style shown to the left is by far the most commonly seen for brochures because it works so well for letter-sized paper, but there are lots of other fold options available. Check with your print shop.

The brochure examples on the following pages are set up for a standard, 8.5 x 11-inch, three-fold brochure like this one.

Tips on designing brochures

Brochures created by new designers have many of the same problems as newsletters: lack of contrast, lack of alignment, and too much Helvetica/Arial. Here's a quick summary of how the principle elements of design can be applied to that brochure you're working on.

Contrast

As in any other design project, contrast not only adds visual interest to a page so a reader's eye is drawn in, but it also helps create the hierarchy of information so the reader can scan the important points and understand what the brochure is about. Use contrast in the typefaces, rules, colors, spacing, size of elements, etc. Remember that the only way contrast is effective is if it's strong—if two elements are not exactly the same, make sure they are **very** different. Otherwise it looks like a mistake. Don't be a wimp.

Repetition

Repeat various elements in the design to create a **unified look** to the piece. You might repeat colors, typefaces, rules, spatial arrangements, bullets, etc.

Alignment

I keep repeating myself about this alignment stuff, but it's important, and the lack of it is consistently a problem. **Strong, sharp edges** create a strong, sharp impression. A combination of alignments (using centered, flush left, and flush right in one piece) usually creates a sloppy, weak impression.

Occasionally, you may want to intentionally break out of the alignment (as I did on the previous page); **this works best if you have other strong alignments** to contrast with the breakout.

Proximity

Proximity, **grouping** similar items close together, is especially important in a project such as a brochure where you have a variety of subtopics within one main topic. How close and how far away items are from each other communicates the relationships of the items.

To create the spatial arrangements effectively, **you must know how to use your software** to create space between the paragraphs (space before or space after) instead of hitting the Enter or Return key twice. Two Returns between paragraphs creates a larger gap than you need, forcing items apart that should be close together. Two Returns also creates the same amount of space *above* a headline or subhead as there is *below* the head (which you don't want), and it separates bulleted items that should be closer together. Learn that software!

Postcards

Because they're so visual and so immediate—no envelopes to fuss with, no paper cuts—postcards are a great way to grab attention. And for these same reasons, an ugly or boring postcard is a waste of everybody's time.

So, to avoid waste, remember the following:

Be different. Oversized or oddly shaped postcards will stand out from that crowd in the mailbox. (Check with the post office, though, to make sure your shape will go through the mail!)

Think "series." A single postcard makes one impression; just think what a series of several could do!

Be specific. Tell the recipient exactly how they'll benefit (and what they need to do to get that benefit).

Keep it brief. Use the front of the postcard for a short and attention-getting message. Put less important details on the back.

If possible, use color. Besides being fun to work with, color attracts the eye and draws interest.

Don't forget: white space is a design element, too!

Don't do this!

What's wrong with this headline?

Don't use 12-point Helvetica, Arial, Times, or Sand.

Don't set information in all caps—it is so difficult to read that few will bother. They didn't ask for the card in the first place, did they?

Use contrast and spatial relationships to communicate a message clearly.

Great GIFT IDEAS for your Internet-obsessed friends

Ratz! That's what you usually say when you realize the holidays are here and you haven't done diddly-squat for shopping. But now when you say "Ratz!" you're reminded of Url Ratz and his Internet Cafe full of unique gifts developed just for Internet mavens like you and your screen-radiated friends and relatives.

Happy Holidays!

Now get on the Internet at www.UrlsInternetCafe.com and do stuff.

The guidelines for business cards (pages 111–114) also apply to postcards: don't stick things in the corners; don't think you have to fill the space; don't make everything the same size or almost the same size.

Try this . . .

Great gift ideas for your Internet-obsessed friends

Ratz! That's what you usually say when you realize the holidays are here and you haven't done diddly-squat for shopping. But now when you say "Ratz!" you're reminded of Url Ratz and his Internet Cafe full of **unique gifts** developed just for Internet mavens like you and your screen-radiated friends and relatives. Happy Holidays.

Now get on the Internet at **UrlsInternetCafe.com** and do stuff.

Try an odd size postcard, such as tall and narrow, short and fat, oversized, or a fold-over card.

Just be sure to take your intended size and paper to the post office and make sure it fits regulations before you print it, or check the web site (usps.gov). And verify the cost of postage for an odd-sized card.

As in any piece where you need to get someone's attention instantly, create a hierarchy of information so the reader can scan the card and make a quick decision as to whether they want to read the rest of it or not.

Great gift ideas for your Internet-obsessed friends

Ratz! That's what you usually say when you realize the holidays are here and and you haven't done diddly-squat for shopping. But now when you say "Ratz!" you're reminded of Url Ratz and his Internet Cafe full of unique gifts developed just for Internet mavens like you and your screen-radiated friends and relatives. Happy Holidays. Now get on the Internet at **UrlsInternetCafe.com** and do stuff.

Tips on designing postcards

You only have a split second to capture someone's attention with an unsolicited postcard that arrives in the mail. No matter how great your copy, if the design of the card does not attract their attention, they won't read your copy.

What's your point?

Your first decision is to determine what sort of effect you want to achieve. Do you want readers to think it is an expensive, exclusive offer? Then your postcard had better look as expensive and professional as the product. Do you want readers to feel like they're getting a great bargain? Then your postcard shouldn't be too slick. Discount stores spend extra money to make their stores look like they contain bargains. It's not an accident that Saks Fifth Avenue has a different look—from the parking lot to the restrooms—than does Kmart, and it doesn't mean that Kmart spent less on decor than did Saks. Each look serves a distinct and definite purpose and reaches out toward a specific market.

Grab their attention

The same design guidelines apply to direct-mail postcards as to anything else: contrast, repetition, alignment, and proximity. But with this kind of postcard, you have very little time to induce recipients into reading it. **Be brave** with bright colors, either in the ink or the card stock. Use striking graphics—there's plenty of great and inexpensive clipart and picture fonts that you can use in all sorts of creative ways.

Contrast

Contrast is probably your best friend in a direct-mail postcard. The headline should be in strong contrast to the rest of the text, the colors should use strong contrast to each other and to the color of the paper stock. And don't forget that **white space** creates contrast!

Newspaper ads

A well-designed newspaper ad can work wonders for an advertiser; however, looking good is not all it takes to be successful in newsprint. Here are a few hints that will help even the sexiest ad rake in results:

White space! Take note of where your eyes go next time you scan the newspaper. Which ads do your eyes naturally land on, and which ads do you actually read? I'll bet you see and read at least the headlines of the ads that have more white space.

Be clever. There's nothing that can compete with a clever headline. Not even good design. (But with both, the possibilities multiply!)

Be clear. Once your catchy headline has garnered some attention, your ad should specifically tell readers what to do (and give them the means to do so; i.e., phone number, email address, web address, etc.).

Be brief. Your ad is not the place to put your life story. Keep the copy simple and to the point.

Use color when you can. It always attracts the eye, particularly when surrounded by a sea of gray text.

wintertime flower sale

Url took care all summer so you could have fresh flowers this winter.

Flowers 2/$5   All day Saturday, January 25   9–6   Url's Internet Cafe

Ads don't have to scream to be effective.

Don't do this!

THIS IS THE TECHNOLOGY AGE. LAB COATS FOR SALE.

You could also use a t-shirt that tells your clients the Internet facts of life. And coffees blended specifically for web surfers.

You'll need matching mugs for the coffee and most likely you'll want original RatPadz© to replace those clunky old mouse pads you have just lying around the office.

Did we mention polo shirts, caps, gift boxes, and do-rags? Prepare yourself for the Technology Age: visit Url's Internet Cafe for great gift ides and a cafe full of educational, fun stuff.

www.UrlsInternetCafe.com

If your headline doesn't grab their attention, they won't read your body copy no matter how big you set it. (If you get rid of the caps, your headline can be set much larger.)

Don't make all the text the same size. Call out your headline, but once you catch the reader's eye and mind with your headline, they will read the rest of the text, even if it's 9-point type.

WOULD YOU BUY A LAB COAT FROM AN UGLY RAT?

You may not think so now, but just wait 'til you see the lab coats, t-shirts, caps, polo shirts, special coffees, teas, mugs, RatPadz©, and other great gift ideas at Url's Internet Cafe.

But people don't come here just to shop. It's a cafe where just hangin' out is an art form. And when that sudden impulse to buy a lab coat hits, we've got 'em right here. So, if you think he's a sleazy, ugly rat, you're right. But come on, how many handsome lab coat salesmen do you know?

www.UrlsInternetCafe.com
P.O. Box 23465
Santa Fe, NM 87505
(505) 424-1115

Don't cram the space full! I know you paid for it, but white space is just as valuable and well worth the money.

Unless your ad offers valuable, free information that a reader really wants to know and can't get anywhere else, don't stuff it. Let there be white space.

Try this . . .

This is the Technology Age.

You need a lab coat.

You could also use a t-shirt that tells
your clients the Internet facts of life
(exhibit A). And coffees blended
specifically for web surfers. You'll need
matching mugs for the coffee and most
likely you'll want original RatPadz©
to replace those clunky old mouse pads
you have just lying around the office.
Did we mention polo shirts, caps, gift boxes, and do-rags?
Prepare yourself for the Technology Age: visit Url's
Internet Cafe for great gift ideas and a cafe full of
educational, fun stuff.

Web site
work is never
done.

(exhibit A)

Url's Internet Cafe

UrlsInternetCafe.com

White space is good.
The trick about white
space is that it needs to be
organized. In the first ad on
the opposite page, there is
just as much white space
as there is in this ad to the
right, but it's sprawled all
over the place.

**Organize the white space
just as consciously as you
organize the information.**
If you follow the other
four principles of design,
the white space will
automatically end up
where it should.

**Would you buy a lab coat
from an
ugly rat?**

You may not think so now,
but just wait 'til you see the
lab coats, t-shirts, caps,
polo shirts, special coffees,
teas, mugs, Ratpadz©, and
other great gift ideas at
Url's Internet Cafe.
But people don't come
here just to shop.
It's a cafe where
just hangin' out
is an art form.
And when that
sudden impulse to
to buy a lab coat hits,
we've got 'em right here.
So, if you think he's a sleazy, ugly rat, you're right. But come on,
how many handsome lab coat salesmen do you know?

Url's Internet Cafe

65 Ratznest Way
Santa Fe, New Mexico
UrlsInternetCafe.com

As with any other
design project, use
contrast, repetition,
alignment, and
proximity. Can you
name where each of
those concepts have
been used in these
ads?

Tips on designing newspaper ads

One of the biggest problems with newspaper ads is crowding. Many clients and businesses who are paying for a newspaper ad feel they need to fill every particle of space because it costs money.

Contrast

With a newspaper ad, you need contrast not only in the advertisement itself, but also between the ad and the rest of the newspaper page that it's placed on. In this kind of ad, the best way to create contrast is with white space. Newspaper pages tend to be completely full of stuff and very busy. An ad that has lots of white space within it stands out on the page, and a reader's eye can't help but be drawn to it. Experiment. Open a newspaper page (or a phone book page) and scan it. I guarantee that if there is white space on that page, your eyes will go to it. They go there because white space provides a strong contrast on a full, busy page.

Once you have white space, your headline doesn't need to be in a big, fat, typeface screaming to compete with everything else. You can actually get away with a beautiful script or a classy oldstyle instead of a heavy face.

Type choices

Newsprint is porous, coarse paper, and the ink spreads on it. So don't use a typeface that has small, delicate serifs or very thin lines that will thicken when printed, unless you are setting the type large enough that the serifs and strokes will hold up.

Reverse type

Avoid reverse type (white type on a dark background) if possible, but if you must have it, make sure you use a good solid typeface with no thin lines that will fill in when the ink spreads. As always when setting type in reverse, use a point size a wee bit larger and bolder than you would if it was not reversed because the optical illusion makes reverse type appear smaller and thinner.

Web sites

While the same four basic principles I've mentioned over and over in this book (contrast, repetition, alignment, proximity) also apply to web design, **repetition** is one of the most important for a web site. The other three principles help the pages look good and make sense, but repetition lets your visitors know whether they're still in the same web site. You should have a consistent navigation system and graphic style so your visitors always know they are in the same web site. Repeating a color scheme, the same typefaces, buttons, or similar-style graphic elements placed in the same position on each page will do the trick.

Designing a web site is quite a bit different from designing printed pieces. If you're brand-new to web design and want to learn how to get started, you really should check out *The Non-Designer's Web Book.*

Your web site should be inviting and easy to move around in. This site is clean and simple.

Google.com is a great example of a fabulous, useful, yet clean and simple site.

Don't do this!

Don't make visitors scroll to see the navigation links!

Don't let text bump up against the left edge of the browser window.

Don't use the default blue color for your text or graphic links. It's a sure sign of an amateur page.

Don't make text links within big, dorky, table cells with the borders turned on.

Don't use bold type for your body copy, and please don't let your body copy run the entire width of the page.

Don't use a fluorescent background color, especially with fluorescent type!

Don't make the visitor scroll sideways!! Keep your page within the 800-pixel width maximum. Especially don't make a table that is wider than 600 pixels or people will be very mad at you when they try to print your page.

Try this . . .

Keep your entry page and your home page within a framework of 800 pixels wide by 600 pixels deep. A visitor should not have to scroll on a home page to find the links!

Absence of the bad features of web design takes you a long way toward good web design.

Take a look at Peachpit.com or Adobe.com. Name at least five things that provide the visitor with a consistent look-and-feel so the visitor always knows, no matter what page they are on, that they are in that site.

Put into words exactly what makes the difference between the examples on these two pages. Naming the design features—both good and bad features—out loud helps you design better.

Tips on designing web pages

Two of the most important factors in good web design are **repetition and clarity/readability.** A visitor should never have to figure out how to use your navigation system, where they are in the site, or whether they are still in your web site or have jumped somewhere else.

Repetition

Repeat certain visual elements on every page in your web site. This not only lets the visitor know they are still at your site, but also provides unity and continuity, intrinsic features of any good design.

Once you get to content pages, the visitor should find the navigation in the same place, in the same order, with the same graphics. Not only does this make it easy for the visitor to find their way through your site, but it provides a **unifying factor** to the collection of pages.

Clarity/Readability

One of the most unreadable places to read text is on a monitor, whether it's television, video, or computer. So we need to make a few adjustments to the text on web pages to make sure it's as easy to read as possible.

Use **shorter line lengths** than you might use on paper. The body copy should never run the entire width of the web page, which means you must put the text in a table or use css code (or at least use a block indent, which indents the text from both the left and right sides). But don't use such short line lengths that you break up the phrasing of the sentences too much.

If you are specifying the text to appear in a certain typeface (if you're not, ignore this), typically Helvetica or Arial and Times or Times Roman, please specify Geneva or Verdana or Trebuchet in front of Helvetica, and New York or Georgia in front of Times. This will make the text on Macintoshes appear so much cleaner and easier to read. (If you use a Mac, set your default font to New York instead of Times, and you will be amazed at how much easier it is to read web pages. Change it back to Times before you print a page.) Verdana and Trebuchet are found on all operating systems updated within the past few years, and they're excellent choices for body copy on the web.

Designing with TYPE

The second half of this book
deals specifically with type,
since type is what design
is all about, yes?
This section particularly
addresses the problem
of combining more than one
typeface on the page.

Although I focus
on the aesthetics of type,
never forget
that your purpose is
communication.
The type should never
inhibit the communication.

typefaces
Miss Fajardose
Tabitha
Onyx

WHAT TYPE SHALL I USE?

The gods refuse
to answer.

They refuse
because
they
do not
know.

W.A. DWIGGINS

typefaces
PERCOLATOR EXPERT
Shannon Book Oblique
ITC Golden Cockerel Initial Ornaments

Type (& Life)

Type is the basic building block of any printed page. Often it is irresistibly compelling and sometimes absolutely imperative to design a page with more than one typeface on it. But how do you know which typefaces work effectively together?

In Life, when there is more than one of anything, a dynamic relationship is established. In Type, there is usually more than one element on a page—even a document of plain body copy typically has heads or subheads or at least page numbers on it. Within these dynamics on the page (or in Life), a relationship is established that is either concordant, conflicting, or contrasting.

> A **concordant** relationship occurs when you use only one type family without much variety in style, size, weight, and so on. It is easy to keep the page harmonious, and the arrangement tends to appear quiet and rather sedate or formal—sometimes downright dull.

> A **conflicting** relationship occurs when you combine typefaces that are *similar* (but not the same) in style, size, weight, and so on. The similarities are disturbing because the visual attractions are not the same (concordant), but neither are they different (contrasting), so they conflict.

> A **contrasting** relationship occurs when you combine separate typefaces and elements that are clearly distinct from each other. The visually appealing and exciting designs that attract your attention typically have a lot of contrast built in, and those contrasts are emphasized.

Most designers tend to wing it when combining more than one typeface on a page. You might have a sense that one face needs to be larger or an element needs to be bolder. However, when you can recognize and *name the contrasts,* you have power over them—you can then get to the root of the conflicting problem faster and find more interesting solutions. And *that* is the point of this section.

Concord

A design is concordant when you choose to use just one face and the other elements on the page have the same qualities as that typeface. Perhaps you use some of the italic version of the font, and perhaps a larger size for a heading, and maybe a graphic or several ornaments— but the basic impression is still concordant.

Most concordant designs tend to be rather calm and formal. This does not mean concord is undesirable—just be aware of the impression you give by using elements that are all in concord with each other.

*L*ife's but a walking shadow, a poor player

that struts and frets his hour upon the stage,

and then is heard no more; it is a tale

told by an idiot, *full of sound and fury,*

signifying nothing.

This concordant example uses Cochin. The first letter is larger and there is some italic type (Cochin Italic), but the entire piece is rather calm and subdued.

typefaces
Cochin Medium *and Italic*

typefaces
Aachen Bold
Linoscript (with Type Embellishments Three)

Hello!

My name is _____

My theme song is _____

When I grow up I want to be _____

The heavy typeface (Aachen Bold) combines well with the heavy border. Even the line for writing on is heavy.

You are cordially invited

to share in our

wedding celebration

Popeye & Olive Oyl

April 1

3 o'clock in the afternoon

Berkeley Square

The typeface (Linoscript), the thin border, and the delicate ornaments all give the same style impression.

Look familiar? Lots of folks play it safe with their wedding invitations by using the principle of concord. That's not a bad thing! But it should be a conscious thing.

Conflict

A design is in conflict when you set two or more typefaces on the same page that are *similar*—not really different and not really the same. I have seen countless students trying to match a typeface with one on the page, looking for a face that "looks similar." Wrong. When you put two faces together that look too much alike without really being so, most of the time it looks like a mistake. *The problem is in the similarities* because the similarities conflict.

Concord is a solid and useful concept; **conflict** should be avoided.

L̲ife's but a walking shadow, a poor player
that struts and frets his hour upon the stage,
and then is heard no more; it is a tale
told by an idiot, **full of sound and fury,**
signifying nothing.

As you read this example, what happens when you get to the phrase, "full of sound and fury"? Do you wonder why it's in another typeface? Do you wonder if perhaps it's a mistake? Does it make you twitch? Does the large initial letter look like it's supposed to be there?

typefaces
Cochin Medium and ITC Garamond Light

typefaces
Bailey Sans Extra Bold and Antique Olive Roman
Linoscript and Shelley Volante Script
Adobe Wood Type Ornaments Two

What's up?

My name is _____

My theme song is _____

When I grow up I want to be _____

Look particularly at the "a," the "t," and the "s" in the headline and the other lines. They are similar but not the same. The border is not the same visual weight as the type or the lines, nor are they in strong contrast. There is too much conflict in this little piece.

You are cordially invited

to share in our

wedding celebration

Popeye & Olive Oyl

April 1

3 o'clock in the afternoon

Berkeley Square

This small invitation uses two different scripts—they have many similarities with each other, but they are not the same and they are not different.

The ornaments have the same type of conflict—too many similarities. The piece looks a bit cluttered.

Contrast

There is no quality in this world that is not what it is merely by contrast. Nothing exists in itself. —Herman Melville

Now this is the fun part. Creating concord is pretty easy, and creating conflict is easy but undesirable. Creating contrast is just fun.

Strong contrast attracts our eyes, as you learned in the previous section about design. One of the most effective, simplest, and satisfying ways to add contrast to a design is with type.

Life's but a walking shadow, a poor player
that struts and frets his hour upon the stage,
and then is heard no more;
it is a tale told by an idiot,

full of sound and fury,

signifying nothing.

In this example it's very clear that the phrase "full of sound and fury" is supposed to be in another typeface. The entire piece of prose has a more exciting visual attraction and a greater energy due to the contrast of type.

typefaces
Cochin Medium and Flyswim

typefaces
Antique Olive Black and Roman
LITHOS EXTRA LIGHT
Zanzibar

Hello!

My name is _____

My theme song is _____

When I grow up I want to be _____

Now the contrast between the typefaces is clear (they are actually in the same family, Antique Olive)—the very bold face contrasts the light face. The line weights of the border and writing lines also have a clear distinction.

YOU ARE CORDIALLY INVITED
TO SHARE IN OUR
WEDDING CELEBRATION!

APRIL 1
3 O'CLOCK
    IN THE AFTERNOON
BERKELEY SQUARE

This invitation uses two very different faces— they are different in many ways.

The font for Popeye and Olive Oyl (called Zanzibar) includes ornaments (one of which is shown here) that work well with the typeface.

Summary

Contrast is not just for the aesthetic look of the piece. It is intrinsically tied in with the organization and clarity of the information on the page. Never forget that your point is to communicate. Combining different typefaces should enhance the communication, not confuse it.

There are six clear and distinct ways to contrast type: size, weight, structure, form, direction, and color. The rest of this book talks about each of these contrasts in turn.

Although I elaborate on each of the contrasts one at a time, rarely is one contrast effective. Most often you will strengthen the effect by combining and emphasizing the differences.

If you have trouble seeing what is wrong with a combination of typefaces, don't look for what is *different* between the faces—look for what is *similar.* It is the similarities that are causing the problem.

The major rule to follow when contrasting type is this: *Don't be a wimp!*

But...

Before we get to the ways to contrast, you need to have a familiarity with the categories of type. Spend a couple of minutes with each page in the next chapter, noting the similarities that unify a category of type. Then try to find a couple of examples of that kind of type before you move on to the next category. Look in magazines, books, on packages, anything printed. Believe me, taking a few moments to do this will make everything sink in so much faster and deeper!

Categories of Type

There are many thousands of different typefaces available right now, and many more are being created every day. Most faces, though, can be dropped into one of the six categories mentioned below. Before you try to become conscious of the *contrasts* in type, you should become aware of the *similarities* between broad groups of type designs, because it is the *similarities* that cause the conflicts in type combinations. The purpose of this chapter is to make you more aware of the details of letterforms. In the following chapter I'll launch into combining them.

Of course, you will find hundreds of faces that don't fit neatly into any category. We could make several hundred different categories for the varieties in type—don't worry about it. The point is just to start looking at type more closely and clearly.

I focus on these six groups:

Oldstyle

Modern

Slab serif

Sans serif

Script

Decorative—INCLUDING GRUNGY!

Oldstyle

Typefaces created in the **oldstyle** category are based on the handlettering of scribes—you can imagine a wedge-tipped pen held in the hand. Oldstyles always have serifs (see the call-out below) and the serifs of lowercase letters are always at an angle (the angle of the pen). Because of that pen, all the curved strokes in the letterforms have a transition from thick to thin, technically called the "thick/thin transition." This contrast in the stroke is relatively moderate, meaning it goes from kind-of-thin to kind-of-thicker. If you draw a line through the thinnest parts of the curved strokes, the line is diagonal. This is called the *stress*—oldstyle type has a diagonal stress.

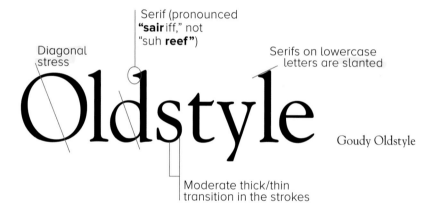

Diagonal stress

Serif (pronounced **"sair** iff," not "suh **reef"**)

Serifs on lowercase letters are slanted

Goudy Oldstyle

Moderate thick/thin transition in the strokes

Goudy   Palatino   Times

Baskerville   Garamond

Do these faces all look pretty much the same to you? Don't worry—they look the same to everyone who hasn't studied typography. Their "invisibility" is exactly what makes oldstyles the best type group for extensive amounts of body copy. There are rarely any distinguishing characteristics that get in the way of reading; they don't call attention to themselves. If you're setting lots of type that you want people to actually read, choose an oldstyle.

Modern

Oldstyle faces replicated the humanist pen stokes. But as history marched on, the structure of type changed. Type has trends and succumbs to lifestyle and cultural changes, just like hairdos, clothes, architecture, or language. In the 1700s, smoother paper, more sophisticated printing techniques, and a general increase in mechanical devices led to type becoming more mechanical also. New typefaces no longer followed the pen in hand. Modern typefaces have serifs, but the serifs are now horizontal instead of slanted, and they are very thin. Like a steel bridge, the structure is severe, with a radical thick/thin transition, or contrast, in the strokes. There is no evidence of the slant of the pen; the stress is perfectly vertical. Moderns tend to have a cold, elegant look.

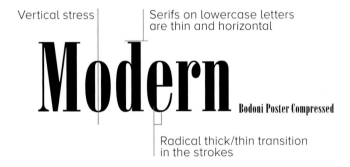

Vertical stress

Serifs on lowercase letters are thin and horizontal

Modern Bodoni Poster Compressed

Radical thick/thin transition in the strokes

Bodoni   **Times Bold**   **Onyx**

Didot, Bold   **Walbaum**

Modern typefaces have a striking appearance, especially when set very large. Because of their strong thick/thin transitions, most moderns are not good choices for extended amounts of body copy—the thin lines almost disappear, the thick lines are prominent, and the effect on the page is called "dazzling."

Slab serif

Along with the industrial revolution came a new concept: advertising. At first, advertisers took modern typefaces and made the thicks thicker. You've seen posters with type like that—from a distance, all you see are vertical lines, like a fence. The obvious solution to this problem was to thicken the entire letterform. Slab serifs have little or no thick/thin transition.

This category of type is sometimes called Clarendon, because the typeface Clarendon (shown below) is the epitome of this style. They are also called Egyptian because they became popular during the Egyptomania craze in Western civilization; many typefaces in this category were given Egyptian names so they would sell (Memphis, Cairo, Scarab).

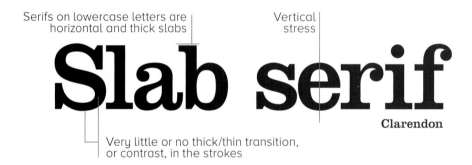

Serifs on lowercase letters are horizontal and thick slabs

Vertical stress

Slab serif

Clarendon

Very little or no thick/thin transition, or contrast, in the strokes

Clarendon   Memphis
New Century Schoolbook
Silica Regular, Light, **Black**

Many of the slab serifs that have a slight thick/thin contrast (such as Clarendon or New Century Schoolbook) are very high on the readability scale, meaning they can easily be used in extensive text. They present an overall darker page than oldstyles, though, because their strokes are thicker and relatively monoweight. Slab serifs are often used in children's books because of their clean, straightforward look.

Sans serif

The word "sans" means "without" (in French), so sans serif typefaces are those without serifs on the ends of the strokes. The idea of removing the serifs was a rather late development in the evolution of type and didn't become wildly successful until the early part of the twentieth century.

Sans serif typefaces are almost always "monoweight," meaning there is virtually no visible thick/thin transition in the strokes; the letterforms are the same thickness all the way around.

Also see the following page for important information on sans serif.

No serifs anywhere

No stress because there's no thick/thin

No thick/thin transition in the strokes

Franklin Gothic

Proxima Nova   Formata

Folio   Shannon Book, **Bold**

Bailey Sans, **Bold**   Syntax

If the only sans serifs you have in your font library are Helvetica/Arial and Avant Garde, the best thing you could do for your pages is invest in a sans serif family that includes a strong, heavy, black face. Each of the families above has a wide variety of weights, from light to extra black. With that one investment, you will be amazed at how your options increase for creating eye-catching pages.

Most sans serifs are monoweight, as shown on the preceding page. A very few, however, have a slight thick/thin transition. Below is an example of Optima, a sans serif with a stress. Faces like Optima are very difficult to combine on a page with other type—they have similarities with serif faces in the thick/thin strokes, and they have similarities with sans serifs in the lack of serifs. Be very careful when working with a sans like this.

Sans serif Optima

Optima is an exceptionally beautiful typeface, but you must be very careful about combining it with other faces. Notice its thick/thin strokes. It has the classic grace of an oldstyle (see page 154), but it's a sans serif.

MAKES YOU THINK ABOUT
YOUR IMMORTALITY.
J. PHILIP DAVIS

Here you see Optima (the smaller text) combined with Tabitha. Tabitha's spunky informality is a nice contrast with Optima's classic grace.

Script

The script category includes all those typefaces that appear to have been handlettered with a calligraphy pen or brush, or sometimes with a pencil or technical pen. This category could easily be broken down into scripts that connect, scripts that don't connect, scripts that look like hand printing, scripts that emulate traditional calligraphic styles, and so on. But for our purposes we are going to lump them all into one pot.

Miss Fajardose   *Arid*   *Ministry Script*

Fountain Pen   *Emily Austin*

Cocktail Shaker

Scripts are like cheesecake—they should be used sparingly so nobody gets sick. The fancy ones, of course, should never be set as long blocks of text and *never* as all caps. But scripts can be particularly stunning when set very large—don't be a wimp!

Carpe Diem

typefaces
Linoscript Medium

Decorative

Decorative fonts are easy to identify —if the thought of reading an entire book in that font makes you wanna throw up, you can probably put it in the decorative pot. Decorative fonts are great—they're fun, distinctive, easy to use, oftentimes cheaper, and there is a font for any whim you wish to express. Of course, simply because they *are* so distinctive, their use is limited.

JUNIPER THE WALL Tabitha

Pious Henry FlySwim Blue Island

FAJITA SCARLETT

When using a decorative typeface, go beyond what you think of as its initial impression. For instance, if Pious Henry strikes you as informal, try using it in a more formal situation and see what happens. If you think Juniper carries a Wild West flavor, try it in a corporate setting or a flower shop and see what happens. Depending on how you use them, decoratives can carry obvious emotions, or you can manipulate them into carrying connotations very different from your first impression. But that is a topic for another book.

Wisdom sometimes benefits from the use of decorative fonts.

Be conscious

To use type effectively, you have to be conscious. By that I mean you must keep your eyes open, you must notice details, you must try to state the problem in words. Or when you see something that appeals to you strongly, put into words *why* it appeals to you.

Spend a few minutes and look through a magazine. Try to categorize the typefaces you see. Many of them won't fit neatly into a single pot, but that's okay—choose the category that seems the closest. The point is that you are looking more closely at letterforms, which is absolutely critical if you are going to combine them effectively.

Little Quiz #3: Categories of type

Draw lines to match the category with the typeface!

Oldstyle	**AT THE RODEO**
Modern	**High Society**
Slab serif	*Too Sassy for Words*
Sans serif	As I remember, Adam
Script	The enigma continues
Decorative	***It's your attitude***

Little Quiz #4: Thick/thin transitions

Do the following typefaces have:

A moderate thick/thin transitions

B radical thick/thin transitions

C no (or negligible) thick/thin transitions

Giggle

A   B   C

Jiggle

A   B   C

Diggle

A   B   C

Piggle

A   B   C

Higgle

A   B   C

Wiggle

A   B   C

Little Quiz #5: Serifs

Do the lowercase letters in the examples below have:

A thin, horizontal serifs

B thick, slabby [hint] horizontal serifs

C no serifs

D slanted serifs

Diggle

A B C D

Riggle

A B C D

Figgle

A B C D

Biggle

A B C D

Miggle

A B C D

Tiggle

A B C D

Notice the huge differences between all the "g" letters! It's too much fun.

Summary

I can't stress enough how important it is that you become conscious of these broad categories of type. As you work through the next chapter, it will become clearer *why* this is important.

A simple exercise to continually hone your visual skills is to collect samples of the categories. Cut them out of any printed material you can find. Do you see any patterns developing within a broad category? Go ahead and make subsets, such as oldstyle typefaces that have small x-heights and tall descenders (see the example below). Or scripts that are really more like hand printing than cursive handwriting. Or extended faces and condensed faces (see below). It is this visual awareness of the letterforms that will give you the power to create interesting, provocative, and effective type combinations.

Bernhard xq
30 point

Baseline.

Ascenders are the parts of letters that are taller than the x-height.

The **x-height** is the height of the main body of the lowercase letters.

Descenders are the parts of letters that are below the **baseline** (the invisible line on which the type sits).

Notice the x-height of Bernhard as compared to Eurostile, below—look at the x-height in relation to the ascenders. Bernhard has an unusually small x-height relative to its ascenders. Most sans serifs have large x-heights. Start noticing those kinds of details.

Eurostile Bold **18 point**   Bernhard 18 point
Eurostile Bold Extended
Eurostile Bold Condensed

Extended typefaces look stretched out; condensed typefaces appear to be squished. Both are appropriate in certain circumstances.

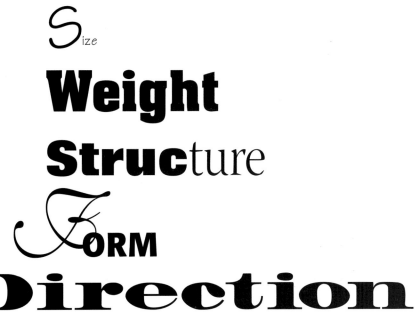

Type Contrasts

This chapter focuses on the topic of combining typefaces. The following pages describe the various ways type can be contrasted. Each page shows specific examples, and at the end of this section are examples using these principles of contrasting type on your pages. Type contrast is not only for the aesthetic appeal, but also to enhance the communication.

A reader should never have to try to figure out what is happening on the page—the focus, the organization of material, the purpose, the flow of information, all should be recognized instantly with a single glance. And along the way, it doesn't hurt to make it beautiful!

These are the contrasts I discuss:

Size

Weight

Structure

*F*ORM

Direction

Color

typefaces
Tekton Regular
Aachen Bold
Folio Extra Bold
& Warnock Pro Regular
Shelley Volante Script
& Formata Bold
Madrone
Zanzibar Regular

 Size

In which category
of type does this
face belong?

A contrast of size is fairly obvious: big type versus little type. To make a contrast of size work effectively, though, *don't be a wimp.* You cannot contrast 12-point type with 14-point type; most of the time they will simply conflict. You cannot contrast 65-point type with 72-point type. If you're going to contrast two typographic elements through their size, *then do it.* Make it obvious—don't let people think it's a mistake.

HEY, SHE'S CALLING YOU A LITTLE

WIMP

Decide on the typographic element that you want seen as a focus. Emphasize it with contrasts.

A N O T H E R

newsletter

Volume 1 ■ Number 1   January ■ 2010

Often other typographic elements have to be there, but aren't really that important to the general reading public. Make them small. Who cares what the volume number is? If someone does care, it can still be read. It's okay not to set it in 12-point type!

typefaces
Folio Light **and Extra Bold**
ITC American Typewriter Medium **and Bold**

A contrast of size does not always mean you must make the type large—it just means there should be a contrast. For instance, when you see a small line of type alone on a large newspaper page, you are compelled to read it, right? An important part of what compels you is the contrast of very small type on that large page.

If you came across this full page in a newspaper, would you read that small type in the middle? Contrast does that.

Sometimes the contrast of big over little can be overwhelming; it can overpower the smaller type. Use that to your advantage. Who wants to notice the word "incorporated" anyway? Although it's small, it's certainly not invisible so it's there for those who need it.

typefaces
Wade Sans Light
DivaDoodles
Brioso Pro
Memphis Extra Bold and Light

Over and over again I have recommended not to use all caps. You probably use all caps sometimes to make the type larger, yes? Ironically, when type is set in all caps, it takes up a lot more space than the lowercase, so you have to make the point size smaller. If you make the text lowercase, you can actually set it in a much larger point size, plus it's more readable.

MERMAID TAVERN

Bread and Friday Streets
Cheapside • London

This title is in 20-point type. That's the largest size
I can use in this space with all caps.

Mermaid Tavern

Bread and Friday Streets
Cheapside • London

typefaces
Silica Bold
Wendy Medium

By making the title lowercase, I could enlarge it to 28-point
type, plus still have room to make it heavier.

Use a contrast of size in unusual and provocative ways. Many of our typographic symbols, such as numbers, ampersands, or quotation marks, are very beautiful when set extremely large. Use them as decorative elements in a headline or a pull quote, or as repetitive elements throughout a publication.

The Sound & the Fury

An unusual contrast of size can become a graphic element in itself—handy if you are limited in the images that are available for a project.

typefaces
Zanzibar Regular
(Zanzibar Regular)

Travel Tips

1 Take twice as much money as you think you'll need.

2 Take half as much clothing as you think you'll need.

3 Don't even bother taking all the addresses of the people who expect you to write.

typefaces
Bodoni Poster
Bauer Bodoni Roman

If you use an item in an unusual size, see if you can repeat that concept elsewhere in the publication to create an attractive and useful repetition.

Weight

In which
category of
type does this
face belong?

The weight of a typeface refers to the thickness of the strokes. Most type families are designed in a variety of weights: regular, bold, perhaps extra bold, semibold, or light. When combining weights, remember the rule: *don't be a wimp.* Don't contrast the regular weight with a semibold—go for the stronger bold. If you are combining type from two different families, one face will usually be bolder than the other—so emphasize it.

Most of the typefaces that come standard with your personal computer are missing a very strong bold in the family. I heartily encourage you to invest in at least one very strong, black face. Look through online type catalogs to find one. A contrast of weight is one of the easiest and most effective ways to add visual interest to a page without redesigning a thing, but you will never be able to get that beautiful, strong contrast unless you have a typeface with big, solid strokes.

Formata Light
Formata Regular
Formata Medium
Formata Bold

Silica Extra Light
Silica Regular
Silica Bold
Silica Black

Garamond Light
Garamond Book
Garamond Bold
Garamond Ultra

These are examples of the various weights that usually come within a family. Notice there is not much contrast of weight between the light and the next weight (variously called regular, medium, or book).

Nor is there a strong contrast between the semibold weights and the bolds. If you are going to contrast with weight, don't be a wimp. If the contrast is not strong, it will look like a mistake.

ANOTHER NEWSLETTER

Headline
Lorem ipsum dolor sit amet, consectetur adips cing elit, diam nonnumy eiusmod tempor incidunt ut lobore et dolore nagna aliquam erat volupat. At enim ad minimim veniami quis nostrud exercitation ullamcorper suscripit laboris nisi ut alquip exea commodo consequat.

Another Headline
Duis autem el eum irure dolor in reprehenderit in voluptate velit esse mol-eratie son conswquat, vel illum dolore en guiat nulla pariatur. At vero esos et accusam et justo odio dis-nissim qui blandit praesent lupatum delenit aigue duos dolor et.

Molestais exceptur sint occaecat cupidat non provident, simil tempor.

Sirt in culpa qui officia deserunt aliquan erat volupat. Lorem ipsum dolor sit amet, consec tetur adipscing elit, diam nonnumy eiusmod tem por incidunt ut lobore

First subhead
Et dolore nagna aliquam erat volupat. At enim ad minimim veni ami quis nostrud exer citation ullamcorper sus cripit laboris nisi ut al quip ex ea commodo consequat.

Duis autem el eum irure dolor in rep rehend erit in voluptate velit esse moles taie son conswquat, vel illum dolore en guiat nulla pariatur. At vero esos et accusam et justo odio disnissim qui blan dit praesent lupatum del enit aigue duos dolor et molestais exceptur sint el eum irure dolor in repre-

Another Newsletter

Headline
Lorem ipsum dolor sit amet, consectetur adips cing elit, diam nonnumy eiusmod tempor incidunt ut lobore et dolore nagna aliquam erat volupat. At enim ad minimim veniami quis nostrud exercitation ullamcorper suscripit laboris nisi ut alquip exea commodo consequat.

Another Headline
Duis autem el eum irure dolor in reprehenderit in voluptate velit esse mol-eratie son conswquat, vel illum dolore en guiat nulla pariatur. At vero esos et accusam et justo odio dis-nissim qui blandit praesent lupatum delenit aigue duos dolor et.

Molestais exceptur sint occaecat cupidat non provident, simil tempor.

Sirt in culpa qui officia deserunt aliquan erat volupat. Lorem ipsum dolor sit amet, consec tetur adipscing elit, diam nonnumy eiusmod tem por incidunt ut lobore

First subhead
Et dolore nagna aliquam erat volupat. At enim ad minimim veni ami quis nostrud exer citation ullamcorper sus cripit laboris nisi ut al quip ex ea commodo consequat.

Duis autem el eum irure dolor in rep rehend erit in voluptate velit esse moles taie son conswquat, vel illum dolore en guiat nulla pariatur. At vero esos et accusam et justo odio disnissim qui blan dit praesent lupatum del enit aigue duos dolor et molestais exceptur sint

Remember these examples in the first part of the book? On the left, I used the fonts that come with the computer; the headlines are Helvetica (Arial) Bold, the body copy is Times Roman Regular.

On the right, the body copy is still Times Roman Regular, but I used a heavier (stronger weight) typeface for the headlines (Aachen Bold). With just that simple change—a heavier weight for contrast—the page is much more inviting to read. (The title is also heavier and is reversed out of a black box, adding contrast.)

Mermaid Tavern

Bread and Friday Streets
Cheapside • London

Remember this example from the previous page? By setting the company name in lowercase instead of all caps, I could not only make the type size larger, but I could make it heavier as well, thus adding more contrast and visual interest to the card. The heavier weight also gives the card a stronger focus.

Not only does a contrast of weight make a page more attractive to your eyes, it is one of the most effective ways of organizing information. You do this already when you make your newsletter headlines and subheads bolder. So take that idea and push it a little harder. Take a look at the table of contents below; notice how you instantly understand the hierarchy of information when key heads or phrases are very bold. This technique is also useful in an index; it enables the reader to tell at a glance whether an index entry is a first-level or a second-level entry, thus eliminating the confusion that often arises when you're trying to look up something alphabetically. Look at the index in this book (or in any of my books).

Contents

Contents

By making the chapter headings bolder, the important information is available at a glance, and there is also a stronger attraction for the eye. Plus it sets up a **repetition** (one of the four main principles of design, remember?). I also added a tiny bit of space **above** each bold heading so the headings would be grouped more clearly with their subheadings (principle of **proximity,** remember?).

typefaces
Warnock Pro Regular
Ronnia Bold

If you have a very gray page and no room to add graphics or to pull out quotes and set them as graphics, try setting key phrases in a strong bold. They will pull the reader into the page. (If you use a bold sans serif within serif body copy, you will probably have to make the bold sans serif a point size smaller to make it appear to be the same size as the serif body copy.)

Wants pawn term dare worsted ladle gull hoe lift wetter murder inner ladle cordage honor itch offer lodge, dock, florist. Disk ladle gull orphan worry putty ladle rat cluck wetter ladle rat hut, an fur disk raisin pimple colder Ladle Rat Rotten Hut.

Wan moaning Ladle Rat Rotten Hut's murder colder inset.

Ladle Rat Rotten Hut, heresy ladle bsking winsome burden barter an shirker cockles. Tick disk ladle basking tutor cordage offer groin-murder hoe lifts honor udder sit offer florist. Shaker lake! Dun stopper laundry wrote! Dun stopper peck floors! Dun daily-doily in ner

florist, an yonder nor sorghum-stenches, dun stopper torque wet no strainers!

Hoe-cake, murder, resplendent Ladle Rat Rotten Hut, and stuttered oft oft. Honor wrote tutor cordage offer groin-murder, Ladle Rat Rotten Hut mitten anomalous woof. Wail, wail, wail, set disk wicket woof, Evanescent Ladle Rat Rotten Hut! Wares are putty ladle gull goring wizard cued ladle basking?

Armor goring tumor oiled groin-murder's, reprisal ladle gull. Grammar's seeking bet. Armor ticking arson burden barter an shirker cockles.

O hoe! Heifer gnats woke, setter wicket woof, butter

taught tomb shelf, Oil tickle shirt court tutor cordage offer groin-murder. Oil ketchup wetter letter, and den—O bore!

Soda wicket woof tucker shirt court, an whinny retched a cordage offer groin-murder, picked inner windrow, an sore debtor pore oil worming worse lion inner bet.

Inner flesh, disk abdominal woof lipped honor bet, paunched honor pore oil worming, any garbled erupt. Den disk ratchet ammonol pot honor groin-murder's nut cup an gnat-gun, any curdled ope inner bet, paunched honor pore oil worming, any garbled erupt. Inner ladle wile, Ladle Rat Rotten Hut a raft

Wants pawn term dare worsted ladle gull hoe lift wetter murder inner ladle cordage honor itch offer lodge, dock, florist. **Disk ladle gull orphan worry putty ladle rat cluck** wetter ladle rat hut, an fur disk raisin pimple colder Ladle Rat Rotten Hut.

Wan moaning Ladle Rat Rotten Hut's murder colder inset.

Ladle Rat Rotten Hut, heresy ladle bsking winsome burden barter an shirker cockles. Tick disk ladle basking tutor cordage offer groin-murder hoe lifts honor udder sit offer florist. Shaker lake! Dun stopper laundry wrote! Dun stopper peck floors!

Dun daily-doily in ner florist, an yonder nor sorghum-stenches, dun stopper torque wet no strainers!

Hoe-cake, murder, resplendent Ladle Rat Rotten Hut, and stuttered oft oft. Honor wrote tutor cordage offer groin-murder, **Ladle Rat Rotten Hut mitten anomalous woof.** Wail, wail, wail, set disk wicket woof, Evanescent Ladle Rat Rotten Hut! Wares are putty ladle gull goring wizard cued ladle basking?

Armor goring tumor oiled groin-murder's, reprisal ladle gull.

wicket woof, butter taught tomb shelf, **Oil tickle shirt court tutor cordage offer groin-murder.** Oil ketchup wetter letter, and den—O bore!

Soda wicket woof tucker shirt court, an whinny retched a cordage offer groin-murder, picked inner windrow, an sore debtor pore oil worming worse lion inner bet.

Inner flesh, disk abdominal woof lipped honor bet, paunched honor pore oil worming, any garbled erupt. **Den disk ratchet ammonol pot honor groin-murder's nut cup an gnat-gun,** any curdled ope inner bet, paunched honor pore oil worming, any garbled erupt. Inner

A completely gray page may discourage a casual reader from perusing the story. With the contrast of bold type, the reader can scan key points and is more likely to delve into the information.

(Sometimes, of course, what a reader wants is a plain gray page. For instance, when you're reading a book, you don't want any fancy type tricks to interrupt your eyes—you just want the type to be invisible. And some magazines and journals prefer the stuffy and formal look of a gray page because their audience feels it imports a more serious impression. There is a place for everything. Just make sure the look you are creating is conscious.)

typefaces
Arno Pro Regular
Bailey Sans Extra Bold

Structure

In which category of type does this face belong?

The structure of a typeface refers to how it is built. Imagine that you were to build a typeface out of material you have in your garage. Some faces are built very monoweight, with almost no discernible weight shift in the strokes, as if you had built them out of tubing (like most sans serifs). Others are built with great emphasis on the thick/thin transitions, like picket fences (the moderns). And others are built in-between. If you are combining type from two different families, *use two families with different structures.*

Remember wading through all that stuff earlier in this section about the different categories of type? Well, this is where it comes in handy. Each of the categories is founded on similar *structures.* So you are well on your way to a type solution if you choose two or more faces from two or more categories.

Ode	Ode	Ode
Ode	Ode	Ode
Ode	Ode	Ode
Ode	Ode	Ode

Little Quiz: Can you name each of the typeface categories represented here (one category per line)?

If not, re-read that section because this simple concept is very important.

Structure refers to how a letter is built, and as you can see in these examples, the structure within each category is quite distinctive.

Robin's Rule: Never put two typefaces from the same category on the same page. There's no way you can get around their similarities. And besides, you have so many other choices—why make life difficult?

Did you read *The Mac is not a typewriter* or *The PC is not a typewriter*? (If you haven't, you should.) In that book I state you should never put two sans serif typefaces on the same page, and you should never put two serif typefaces on the same page—*until you have had some typographic training.* Well, this is your typographic training—you are now qualified and licensed to put two sans serifs or two serifs on the same page.

The law is, though, that you must pull two faces from two different categories of type. That is, you can use two serifs as long as one is an oldstyle and the other is a modern or a slab serif. Even then you must be careful and you must emphasize the contrasts, but it *is* perfectly possible to make it work.

Along the same line, avoid setting two oldstyles on the same page—they have too many similarities and are guaranteed to conflict no matter what you do. Avoid setting two moderns, or two slabs, for the same reason. Avoid using two scripts on the same page.

You can't let

the seeds

stop you

from enjoying

the watermelon.

There are five different typefaces in this one little quote. They don't look too bad together because of one thing: they each have a different structure; **they are each from a different category of type.**

typefaces
Formata Bold (sans serif)
Bauer Bodoni Roman (modern)
Blackoak (slab serif)
Goudy Oldstyle (oldstyle)
Shelley Volante (script)

Form

In which category
of type does this
face belong?

The form of a letter refers to its shape. Characters may have the same structure, but different "forms." For instance, a capital letter "G" has the same *structure* as a lowercase letter "g" in the same family. But their actual *forms,* or shapes, are very different from each other. An easy way to think of a contrast of form is to think of caps versus lowercase.

G g

A a

B b

H h

E e

The **forms** of each of these capital letters (Warnock Pro Light Display) are distinctly different from the **forms, or shapes,** of the lowercase letters. So caps versus lowercase is another way to contrast type.

This is something you've probably been doing already, but now, being more conscious of it, you can take greater advantage of its potential for contrast.

In addition to each individual capital letterform being different from its lowercase form, the form of the entire all-cap word is also different. This is what makes all caps so difficult to read. We recognize words not only by their letters, but by their forms, the shapes of the entire words. All words that are set in capital letters have a similar rectangular form, as shown below, and we are forced to read the words letter by letter.

You're probably tired of hearing me recommend not using all caps. I don't mean *never* use all caps. All caps are not *impossible* to read, obviously. Just be conscious of their reduced legibility and readability. Sometimes you can argue that the design "look" of your piece justifies the use of all caps, and that's okay! You must also accept, however, that the words are not as easy to read. If you can consciously state that the lower readability is worth the design look, then go ahead and use all caps.

Every word in all caps has the same form: rectangular.

Caps versus lowercase (contrast of form) usually needs strengthening with other contrasts. Size is the only other contrast added in this example.

Another clear contrast of form is roman versus italic. Roman, in any typeface, simply means that the type stands straight up and down, as opposed to italic or script, where the type is slanted and/or flowing. Setting a word or phrase in italic to gently emphasize it is a familiar concept that you already use regularly.

G g nerdette

G g nerdette

The first line is roman type; the second line is italic. They are both Brioso Pro; their **structures** are exactly the same, but their **forms (shapes)** are different.

Be far flung away

Be far flung away

Particularly notice that "true-drawn" italic (first line) is not simply slanted roman (second line). The true-drawn italic letterforms have actually been redrawn into different shapes. Look carefully at the differences between the e, f, a, g, and y (both lines use the same font).

Be far flung away

Be far flung away

Sans serifs faces usually (not always) have "oblique" versions, which look like the letters are just tilted. Most sans serif roman and oblique forms are not so very different from each other.

"Yes, oh, *yes,*" she chirped.

"Yes, oh, *yes,*" she chirped.

Which of these two sentences contains a word in fake italic?

Since all scripts and italics have a slanted and/or flowing form, it is important to remember to never combine two different italic fonts, or two different scripts, or an italic with a script. Doing so will invariably create a conflict—there are too many similarities. Fortunately, it's not difficult to find great fonts to combine with scripts or italics.

Work Hard
There is no shortcut.

So what do you think about these two typefaces together? Is something wrong? Does it make you twitch? One of the problems with this combination is that both faces have the same form—they both have a cursive, flowing form. One of the fonts has to change. To what? (Think about it.)

Yes—one face has to change to some sort of roman. While we're changing it, we might as well make the **structure** of the new typeface very different also, instead of one with a thick/thin contrast. And we can make it heavier as well.

Work Hard
there is no shortcut

typefaces

Charme
Goudy Oldstyle Italic
Aachen Bold

Direction

In which category of type does this face belong?

An obvious interpretation of type "direction" is type on a slant. Since this is so obvious, the only thing I want to say is don't do it. Well, you might want to do it sometimes, but only do it if you can state in words why this type must be on a slant, why it enhances the aesthetics or communication of the piece. For instance, perhaps you can say, "This notice about the boat race really should go at an angle up to the right because that particular angle creates a positive, forward energy on the page." Or, "The repetition of this angled type creates a staccato effect which emphasizes the energy of the Bartok composition we are announcing." But please, never fill the corners with angled type.

Type slanting upward to the right creates a positive energy. Type slanting downward creates a negative energy. Occasionally you can use these connotations to your advantage.

Sometimes a strong re-direction of type creates a dramatic impact or a unique format— which is a good justification for its use.

the shakespeare papers

Amusing, Tantalizing, and Educative

Lorem ipsum dolor sit amet, consectetur adips cing elit, diam nonnumy eiusmod tempor incidunt ut lobore et dolore nagna aliquam erat volupat. At enim ad minimim veniami quis nos trud ex ercitation ullamcorper sus cripit laboris nisi ut alquip exea commodo consequat.

Unexpected

Duis autem el eum irure dolor in reprehenderit in volu ptate velit esse mol eratie son conswquat, vel illum dolore en guiat nulla pariatur. At vero esos et accusam et justo odio disnissim qui blandit pra esent lupatum delenit ai gue duos dolor et. Molestais

exceptur sint occaecat cupidat non pro vident, simil tempor. Sirt in culpa qui officia des erunt aliquan erat volupat. Lorem ipsum dolor sit amet, consec tetur adip scing elit, diam no numy eiusmod tem por incidunt ut lobore.

Intriguing and Controversial

Et dolore nagna aliquam erat volupat. At enim ad minimim veni ami quis nostrud exer citation ulla mcorper sus cripit laboris nisi ut al quip ex ea commodo consequat.

Duis autem el eum irure dolor in rep rehend erit in proles to maheminit and smit off their heads forthwith.

VOLUPTATE VELIT ESSE moles taie son conswquat, vel illum dolore en guiat nulla pariatur. At vero esos et accusam et justo odio disnissim qui blan dit praesent lupatum del enit aigue duos dolor et mol estais exceptur sint. El eum irure dolor in rep rehend erit in voluptate. At enim ad minimim veniami quis nostrud ex ercitation ullamcorper sus cripit laboris nisi ut alquip exea commodo consequat. Et dolore nagna aliquam erat volupat. At enim ad minimim veni ami quis nostrud exer citation ulla mcorper sus cripit laboris nisi ut al quip ex ea commodo consequat. Vero esos et accusam et justo odio disnissim qui blan dit praesent.

typefaces
Fountain Pen
Formata Light **and Bold**
Brioso Pro Caption

But there is another form of "direction." Every element of type has a direction, even though it may run straight across the page. A *line* of type has a horizontal direction. A tall, thin *column* of type has a vertical direction. It is these more sophisticated directional movements of type that are fun and interesting to contrast. For instance, a double-page spread with a bold headline running across the two pages and the body copy in a series of tall, thin columns creates an interesting contrast of direction.

Experience

teaches

you to

recognize

a mistake—

when

you've

made it

again.

If you have a layout that has the potential for a contrast of direction, emphasize it. Perhaps use an extended typeface in the horizontal direction, and a tall typeface in the vertical direction. Emphasize the vertical by adding extra linespace, if appropriate, and narrower columns than you perhaps originally planned on.

typefaces
Sneakers UltraWide
Coquette Regular
Adobe Wood Type Ornaments Two

You can involve other parts of your layout in the contrast of type direction, such as graphics or lines, to emphasize or contrast the direction.

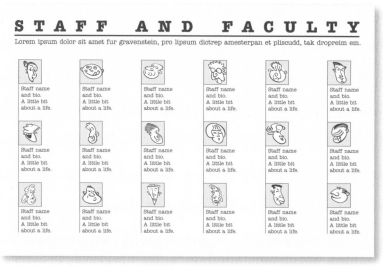

Long horizontals and tall, thin columns can be combined in an endless variety of elegant layouts. Alignment is a key factor here—strong visual alignments will emphasize and strengthen the contrasts of direction.

typefaces
ITC American Typewriter
Medium **and Bold**
MiniPics HeadBuddies: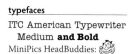

In this example, the direction of the text provides a counter-balance to a horizontal image.

typefaces
Industria Solid
Cotoris Bold

In the example below, there is a nice, strong contrast of direction. But what other contrasts have also been employed to strengthen the piece? There are three different typefaces in that arrangement—*why* do they work together?

Also notice the texture that is created from the structures of the various typefaces, their linespacing, their letterspacing, their weight, their size, their form. If the letters were all raised and you could run your fingers over them, each contrast of type would also give you a contrast of texture—you can "feel" this texture visually. This is a subtle, yet important, part of type. Various textures will occur automatically as you employ other contrasts, but it's good to be conscious of texture and its effect.

MARY SIDNEY
COUNTESS OF PEMBROKE

IF IT'S BEEN
SAID IN
ENGLISH,
MARY
SAID IT
BETTER.

Ay me, to whom shall I my case complain that may compassion my impatient grief? Or where shall I unfold my inward pain, that my enriven heart may find relief?

To heavens? Ah, they alas the authors were, and workers of my unremedied woe: for they foresee what to us happens here, and they foresaw, yet suffered this be so.

To men? Ah, they alas like wretched be, and subject to the heavens ordinance: Bound to abide what ever they decree, their best redress is their best sufferance.

Then to my self will I my sorrow mourn, since none alive like sorrowful remains, and to my self my plaints shall back return, to pay their usury with doubled pains.

Spend a few minutes to put into words why these three typefaces work together.

If you choose a modern in all caps for the headline, what would be a logical choice for body text?

If you had, instead, chosen a modern typeface for the short quote, what would then be a logical choice for the headline?

typefaces
Bodoni Poster Compressed
Eurostile Bold Extended 2
ITC American Typewriter Medium

Color

In which category of type does this face belong?

Color is another term, like direction, with obvious interpretations. When you're talking about actual color, remember to keep in mind that warm colors (reds, oranges) come forward and command our attention. Our eyes are very attracted to warm colors, so it takes very little red to create a contrast. Cool colors (blues, greens), on the other hand, recede from our eyes. You can get away with larger areas of a cool color; in fact, you *need* more of a cool color to create an effective contrast.

Scarlett
FLORENCE

Notice that even though the name "Scarlett" is much smaller, it competes with the larger word because of the warm color.

Now the larger name in the warm color overpowers the smaller name. You usually want to avoid this—or take advantage of it.

Notice how the light blue "Scarlett" almost disappears.

Scarlett
FLORENCE

To contrast with a cool color effectively, you generally need to use more of it.

typefaces
Shelley Volante Scripte
Goudy Oldstyle

But typographers have always referred to **black-and-white type** on a page as having **color.** It's easy to create contrast with "colorful" colors; it takes a more sophisticated eye to see and take advantage of the color contrasts in black-and-white.

In the quote below, you can easily see different "colors" in the black and white text.

"Color" is created by such variances as the weight of the letterforms, the structure, the form, the space inside the letters, the space between the letters, the space between the lines, the size of the type, or the size of the x-height. Even within one typeface, you can create different colors.

Just as the voice adds emphasis
to important words, so can type:
**it shouts or whispers
by variation of size.**

Just as the pitch of the voice adds
interest to the words, so can type:
**it modulates by lightness
or darkness.**

Just as the voice adds color to the
words by inflection, so can type:
**it defines elegance,
dignity, toughness
by choice of face.**

Jan V. White

Squint your eyes and look at this. Get used to considering the different values of blocks of text as having "color."

typefaces
Cochin Medium *and Italic*
Eurostile Bold Extended 2

A light, airy typeface with lots of letterspacing and linespacing creates a very light color (and texture). A bold sans serif, tightly packed, creates a dark color (with a different texture). This is a particularly useful contrast to employ on those text-heavy pages where there are no graphics.

A gray, text-only page can be very dull to look at and uninviting to read. It can also create confusion: in the example below, are these two stories related to each other?

Ladle Rat Rotten Hut

Wants pawn term dare worsted ladle gull hoe lift wetter murder inner ladle cordage honor itch offer lodge, dock, florist. Disk ladle gull orphan worry Putty ladle rat cluck wetter ladle rat hut, an fur disk raisin pimple colder Ladle Rat Rotten Hut.

Wan moaning Ladle Rat Rotten Hut's murder colder inset. "Ladle Rat Rotten Hut, heresy ladle basking winsome burden barter an shirker cockles. Tick disk ladle basking tutor cordage offer groin-murder hoe lifts honor udder site offer florist. Shaker lake! Dun stopper laundry wrote! Dun stopper peck floors! Dun daily-doily inner florist, an yonder nor sorghum-stenches, dun stopper torque wet strainers!"

"Hoe-cake, murder," resplendent Ladle Rat Rotten Hut, an tickle ladle basking an stuttered oft. Honor wrote tutor cordage offer groin-murder, Ladle Rat Rotten Hut mitten anomalous woof.

"Wail, wail, wail!" set disk wicket woof, "Evanescent Ladle Rat Rotten Hut! Wares are putty ladle gull goring wizard ladle basking?"

"Armor goring tumor groin-murder's," reprisal ladle gull. "Grammar's seeking bet. Armor ticking arson burden barter an shirker cockles."

"O hoe! Heifer gnats woke," setter wicket woof, butter taught tomb shelf, "Oil tickle shirt court tutor cordage offer groin-murder. Oil ketchup wetter letter, an den—O bore!"

Soda wicket woof tucker shirt court, an whinny retched a cordage offer groin-murder, picked inner windrow, an sore debtor pore oil worming worse lion inner bet. Inner flesh, disk abdominal woof lipped honor bet, paunched honor pore oil worming, an garbled erupt. Den disk ratchet ammonol pot honor groin-murder's nut cup an gnat-gun, any curdled ope inner bet.

Inner ladle wile, Ladle Rat Rotten Hut a raft attar cordage, an ranker dough ball. "Comb ink, sweat hard," setter wicket woof, disgracing is verse. Ladle Rat Rotten Hut entity bet rum, an stud buyer groin-murder's bet.

"O Grammar!" crater ladle gull historically, "Water bag icer gut! A nervous sausage bag ice!"

"Battered lucky chew whiff, sweat hard," setter bloat-Thursday woof, wetter wicket small honors phase.

"O, Grammar, water bag noise! A nervous sore suture anomalous prognosis!"

"Battered small your whiff, doling," whiskered dole woof, ants mouse worse waddling.

"O Grammar, water bag mouser gut! A nervous sore suture bag mouse!"

Daze worry on-forger-nut ladle gull's lest warts. Oil offer sodden, caking offer carvers an sprinkling otter bet, disk hoard-hoarded woof lipped own pore Ladle Rat Rotten Hut an garbled erupt.

Mural: Yonder nor sorghum stenches shut ladle gulls stopper torque wet strainers.

—H. Chace
Anguish Languish

Old Singleton

. . . Singleton stood at the door with his face to the light and his back to the darkness. And alone in the dim emptiness of the sleeping forecastle he appeared bigger, colossal, very old; old as Father Time himself, who should have come there into this place as quiet as a sepulcher to contemplate with patient eyes the short victory of sleep, the consoler. Yet he was only a child of time, a lonely relic of a devoured and forgotten generation. He stood, still strong, as ever unthinking; a ready man with a vast empty past and with no future, with his childlike impulses and his man's passions already dead within his tattooed breast.

—Joseph Conrad

This might be a typical page in a newsletter or other publication. The monotonous gray does not attract your eye; there's no enticement to dive in and read.

typefaces
Warnock Pro Regular *and Italic*

If you add some "color" to your heads and subheads with a stronger weight, or perhaps set a quote, passage, or short story in an obviously different "color," then readers are more likely to stop on the page and actually read it. And that's our point, right?

Besides making the page more inviting to read, this change in color also helps organize the information. In the example below, it is now clearer that there are two separate stories on the page.

Ladle Rat Rotten Hut

Wants pawn term dare worsted ladle gull hoe lift wetter murder inner ladle cordage honor itch offer lodge, dock, florist. Disk ladle gull orphan worry Putty ladle rat cluck wetter ladle rat hut, an fur disk raisin pimple colder Ladle Rat Rotten Hut.

Wan moaning Ladle Rat Rotten Hut's murder colder inset. "Ladle Rat Rotten Hut, heresy ladle basking winsome burden barter an shirker cockles. Tick disk ladle basking tutor cordage offer groin-murder hoe lifts honor udder site offer florist. Shaker lake! Dun stopper laundry wrote! Dun stopper peck floors! Dun daily-doily inner florist, an yonder nor sorghum-stenches, dun stopper torque wet strainers!"

"Hoe-cake, murder," resplendent Ladle Rat Rotten Hut, an tickle ladle basking an stuttered oft. Honor wrote tutor cordage offer groin-murder, Ladle Rat Rotten Hut mitten anomalous woof.

"Wail, wail, wail!" set disk wicket woof, "Evanescent Ladle Rat Rotten Hut! Wares are putty ladle gull goring wizard ladle basking?"

"Armor goring tumor groin-murder's," reprisal ladle gull. "Grammar's seeking bet. Armor ticking arson burden barter an shirker cockles."

"O hoe! Heifer gnats woke," setter wicket woof, butter taught tomb shelf, "Oil tickle shirt court tutor cordage offer groin-murder. Oil ketchup wetter letter, an den—O bore!"

Soda wicket woof tucker shirt court, an whinny retched a cordage offer groin-murder, picked inner windrow, an sore debtor pore oil worming worse lion inner bet. Inner flesh, disk abdominal woof lipped honor bet, paunched honor pore oil worming, an garbled erupt. Den disk ratchet ammonol pot honor groin-murder's nut cup an gnat-gun, any curdled ope inner bet.

Inner ladle wile, Ladle Rat Rotten Hut a raft attar cordage, an ranker dough ball. "Comb ink, sweat hard," setter wicket woof, disgracing is verse. Ladle Rat Rotten Hut entity bet rum, an stud buyer groin-murder's bet.

"O Grammar!" crater ladle gull historically, "Water bag icer gut! A nervous sausage bag ice!"

"Battered lucky chew whiff, sweat hard," setter bloat-Thursday woof, wetter wicket small honors phase.

"O, Grammar, water bag noise! A nervous sore suture anomalous prognosis!"

"Battered small your whiff, doling," whiskered dole woof, ants mouse worse waddling.

"O Grammar, water bag mouser gut! A nervous sore suture bag mouse!"

Daze worry on-forger-nut ladle gull's lest warts. Oil offer sodden, caking offer carvers an sprinkling otter bet, disk hoard-hoarded woof lipped own pore Ladle Rat Rotten Hut an garbled erupt.

Mural: Yonder nor sorghum stenches shut ladle gulls stopper torque wet strainers.
—H. Chace, *Anguish Languish*

Old Singleton

. . . Singleton stood at the door with his face to the light and his back to the darkness. And alone in the dim emptiness of the sleeping forecastle he appeared bigger, colossal, very old; old as Father Time himself, who should have come there into this place as quiet as a sepulcher to contemplate with patient eyes the short victory of sleep, the consoler. Yet he was only a child of time, a lonely relic of a devoured and forgotten generation. He stood, still strong, as ever unthinking; a ready man with a vast empty past and with no future, with his childlike impulses and his man's passions already dead within his tattooed breast. —Joseph Conrad

This is the same layout, but with added "color." Also, look again at many of the other examples in this book and you'll often see contrasting typefaces that create variations in color.

typefaces
Aachen Bold
Warnock Pro Caption and Light Italic Caption
Eurostile Extended 2 **and Demi**

Below, notice how you can change the color in one typeface, one size, with minor adjustments. As you can see, these minor adjustments can also affect how many words fit into a space.

Center Alley worse jester pore ladle gull hoe lift wetter stop-murder an toe heft-cisterns. Daze worming war furry wicket an shellfish parsons, spatially dole stop-murder, hoe dint lack Center Alley an, infect, word	9 point Warnock Regular, 10.6 leading.
Center Alley worse jester pore ladle gull hoe lift wetter stop-murder an toe heft-cisterns. Daze worming war furry wicket an shellfish parsons, spatially dole stop-murder, hoe dint lack	9 point Warnock Bold, 10.6 leading. This is exactly the same as the example above, except it is the Bold version.
Center Alley worse jester pore ladle gull hoe lift wetter stop-murder an toe heft-cisterns. Daze worming war furry wicket an shellfish parsons, spatially dole stop-murder, hoe dint lack Center Alley an, infect, word orphan traitor pore gull mar lichen	9 point Warnock Light, 10.6 leading. This is exactly the same as the first example above, except it is the Light version of the font, not the Regular.
Center Alley worse jester pore ladle gull hoe lift wetter stop-murder an toe heft-cisterns. Daze worming war furry wicket an shellfish parsons, spatially dole stop-murder, hoe dint lack	9 point Warnock Light, 13 leading, extra letterspacing. Notice it has a lighter color than the example above (same font) due to the extra space between the lines (the leading) and the letters.
Center Alley worse jester pore ladle gull hoe lift wetter stop-murder an toe heft-cisterns. Daze worming war furry wicket an shellfish parsons, spatially dole stop-murder, hoe dint lack Center	9 point Warnock Light Italic, 13 leading, extra letterspacing. This is exactly the same as the one above, except italic. It has a different color and texture.

Below you see just plain examples of typeface color, without any of the extra little manipulations you can use to change the type's natural color. Most good type books display a wide variety of typefaces in blocks of text so you can see the color and texture on the page. An excellent type specimen book from a type vendor might show you each face in a block of text for color comparisons, or you can make your own on your computer.

Center Alley worse jester pore ladle gull hoe lift wetter stop-murder an toe heft-cisterns. Daze worming war furry wicket an shellfish parsons, spatially dole stop-murder, hoe dint lack Center Alley an, infect, word

American Typewriter, 8/10

Center Alley worse jester pore ladle gull hoe lift wetter stop-murder an toe heft-cisterns. Daze worming war furry wicket an shellfish parsons, spatially dole stop-murder, hoe dint lack Center Alley an, infect, word orphan traitor pore gull mar lichen ammonol dinner hormone bang.

Bernhard Modern, 8/10

Center Alley worse jester pore ladle gull hoe lift wetter stop-murder an toe heft-cisterns. Daze worming war furry wicket an shellfish parsons, spatially dole stop-murder, hoe dint lack Center Alley an, infect, word orphan traitor pore gull mar lichen ammonol dinner hormone bang.

Imago, 8/10

Center Alley worse jester pore ladle gull hoe lift wetter stop-murder an toe heft-cisterns. Daze worming war furry wicket an shellfish parsons, spatially dole stop-murder, hoe dint lack Center Alley an, infect, word orphan traitor pore gull mar lichen ammonol dinner hormone bang.

Memphis Medium, 8/10

Center Alley worse jester pore ladle gull hoe lift wetter stop-murder an toe heft-cisterns. Daze worming war furry wicket an shellfish parsons, spatially dole stop-murder, hoe dint lack Center Alley an, infect, word orphan traitor pore gull mar lichen ammonol dinner hormone bang.

Photina, 8/10

Center Alley worse jester pore ladle gull hoe lift wetter stop-murder an toe heft-cisterns. Daze worming war furry wicket an shellfish parsons, spatially dole stop-murder, hoe dint lack Center Alley

Eurostile Extended, 8/10

Combine the contrasts

Don't be a wimp. Most effective type layouts take advantage of more than one of the contrasting possibilities. For instance, if you are combining two serif faces, each with a different structure, emphasize their differences by contrasting their form also: if one element is in roman letters, all caps, set the other in italic, lowercase. Contrast their size, too, and weight; perhaps even their direction. Take a look at the examples in this section again—each one uses more than one principle of contrast.

For a wide variety of examples and ideas, take a look through any good magazine. Notice that every one of the interesting type layouts depends on the contrasts. Subheads or initial caps emphasize the contrast of size with the contrast of weight; often, there is also a contrast of structure (serif vs. sans serif) and form (caps vs. lowercase) as well.

Try to verbalize what you see. *If you can put the dynamics of the relationship into words, you have power over it.* When you look at a type combination that makes you twitch because you have an instinctive sense that the faces don't work together, analyze it with words.

Before trying to find a better solution, you must find the problem. To find the *problem,* try to name the *similarities*—not the differences. What is it about the two faces that compete with each other? Are they both all caps? Are they both typefaces with a strong thick/thin contrast in their strokes? How effective is their contrast of weight? Size? Structure?

Or perhaps the focus conflicts—is the *larger* type a *light* weight and the *smaller* type a *bold* weight, making them fight with each other because each one is trying to be more important than the other?

Name the problem, then you can create the solution.

Summary

This is a list of the contrasts I discussed. You might want to keep this list visible for when you need a quick bang-on-the-head reminder.

Size   Don't be a wimp.

Weight   Contrast heavy weights with light weights, not medium weights.

Structure   Look at how the letterforms are built—monoweight or thick/thin.

**ORM**   Caps versus lowercase is a contrast of form, as well as roman versus italic or script. Scripts and italics have similar forms—don't combine them.

Direction

Think more in terms of horizontal type versus tall, narrow columns of type, rather than type on a slant.

Color   Warm colors come forward; cool colors recede. Experiment with the "colors" of black text.

Little Quiz #6: Contrast or conflict

Look carefully at each of the following examples. Decide whether the type combinations **contrast** effectively, or if there is a **conflict** going on. **State why the combination of faces works** (look for the differences), **or state why it doesn't** (look for the similarities). [Ignore the words themselves—don't get wrapped up in whether the typeface is appropriate for its product, because that's another topic altogether. *Just look at the typefaces.*] If this is your book, circle the correct answers.

contrasts
conflicts

FANCY
PERFUME

contrasts
conflicts

extremely good
DOGFOOD

contrasts
conflicts

MY MOTHER
This is an essay on why my Mom will always be the greatest mother in the world. Until I turn into a teenager.

contrasts
conflicts

FUNNY FARM
Health Insurance

contrasts
conflicts

let's***DANCE***tonight

Little Quiz #7: Dos and don'ts

Rather than give you a list of **do**s and **don't**s, I'm going to let you decide what should and should not be done. Circle the correct answers.

1 Do Don't Use two scripts on the same page.

2 Do Don't Use two moderns, two sans serifs, two oldstyles, or two slab serifs on the same page.

3 Do Don't Add importance to one typographic element by making it bolder, and to another on the same page by making it bigger.

4 Do Don't Use a script and an italic on the same page.

5 Do Don't If one face is tall and slender, choose another face that is short and thick.

6 Do Don't If one face has strong thick/thin transitions, choose a sans serif or a slab serif.

7 Do Don't If you use a very fancy decorative face, find another fancy, eye-catching typeface to complement it.

8 Do Don't Create a type arrrangement that is extremely interesting, but unreadable.

9 Do Don't Remember the four basic principles of design when using any type in any way.

10 Do Don't Break the rules, *once you can name them.*

An exercise in combining contrasts

Here is a fun exercise that is easy to do and will help fine-tune your typographic skills. All you need is tracing paper, a pen or pencil (the little colorful plastic-tip markers are great for this), and a magazine or two.

Trace any word in the magazine that appeals to you. Now find another word in the magazine that creates an effective contrast with the one you just traced. In this exercise, the words are completely irrelevant—you are looking just at letterforms. Here is an example of a combination of three faces that I traced out of a news magazine:

The first word I traced was "Hawk." Once I did that, I didn't even have to look at any more sans serifs. "Rebate" has a very different form from "hawk," and I needed something small and light and with a different structure as a third face.

Trace the first word, and then make a conscious, verbal decision as to what you need to combine with that word. For instance, if the first word or phrase is some form of sans serif, you know that whatever you choose next won't be another sans serif, right? What *do* you need? Put your choices into conscious thoughts.

Try a few combinations of several words, then try some other projects, such as a report cover, a short story on one page with an interesting title, a newsletter masthead, a magazine cover, an announcement, and anything else that may be pertinent to you. Try some colored pens, also. Remember, the words don't have to make any sense at all.

The advantage of tracing from magazines is that you have an abundance of different typefaces that you probably don't have on your computer. Is this going to make you lust after more typefaces? Yes.

So, Does it Make Sense?

Is all this making sense to you? Once you see it, it seems so simple, doesn't it? It won't take long before you won't even have to think about the ways to contrast type—you will just automatically reach for the right typeface. That is, if you have the right typeface in your computer. Fonts (typefaces) are so inexpensive right now, and you really only need a few families with which to make all sorts of dynamic combinations—choose one family from each category, making sure the sans serif family you choose contains a heavy black as well as a very light weight.

And then go to it. And have fun!

The process

Where do you begin when you start to design or re-design something?

Start with the focal point. Decide what it is you want readers to see first. Unless you have chosen to create a very concordant design, create your focal point with strong contrasts.

Group your information into logical groups; decide on the relationships between these groups. Display those relationships with the closeness or lack of closeness **(proximity)** of the groups.

As you arrange the type and graphics on the page, **create and maintain strong alignments.** If you see a strong edge, such as a photograph or vertical line, strengthen it with the alignments of other text or objects.

Create a repetition, or find items that can have a repetitive connection. Use a bold typeface or a rule or a dingbat or a spatial arrangement. Take a look at what is already repeated naturally, and see if it would be appropriate to add more strength to it.

Unless you have chosen to create a concordant design, make sure you have **strong contrasts** that will attract a reader's eye. Remember—contrast is *contrast.* If *everything* on the page is big and bold and flashy, then there is no contrast! Whether it is contrasting by being bigger and bolder or by being smaller and lighter, the point is that it is different and so your eye is attracted to it.

An exercise

Open your local newspaper or telephone book yellow pages. Find any advertisement that you know is not well-designed (especially with your newly heightened visual awareness). You won't have any trouble finding several, I'm sure.

Take a piece of tracing paper and trace the outline of the ad (no fair making it bigger). Now, moving that piece of tracing paper around, trace other parts of the ad, but put them where they belong, giving them strong alignments, putting elements into closer proximity where appropriate, making sure the focal point is really a focal point. Change the capital letters into lowercase, make some items bolder, some smaller, some bigger, get rid of obviously useless junk.

Tip: The neater you do this, the more impressive the result. If you just scratch it on, your finished piece won't look any better than the original.

(And that's a trick I taught my graphic design students—whenever you have a client who insists on his own dorky design and doesn't want to think seriously about your more sophisticated work, make your rendering of his design a little messy. Spill some coffee on it, let the edges get raggedy, smear the pencil around, don't line things up, etc. For the designs that you know are much better, do them brilliantly clean and neat, print them onto excellent paper, mount them onto illustration board, cover them with a protective flap, etc. Most of the time the client will think lo and behold your work really does look better than his original concept, and since he is a VIP* (which you are no longer), he won't be able to pinpoint why his doesn't look so good anymore. His impression is that yours looks better. And don't you dare tell anybody I told you this.)

*VIP: visually illiterate person

Okay—redesign this!

Here's a little poster. Not too bad—though it could use a little help. A few simple changes will make a world of difference. Its biggest problem is the lack of a strong alignment, plus there are several different elements competing for the focal point. Use tracing paper to rearrange elements, or sketch a few versions right onto this page.

Url's Training Camp

Get on the Internet and do stuff!

Join Url for a weekend
of training in the high
desert of Santa Fe.

Workshops in:
Web design and CSS
Keywords
Searching
Blogging and podcasting

**Friday, Saturday, Sunday
First weekend in May**

Answers to Quizzes

As a college teacher, all the quizzes, tests, and projects I give are "open book, open mouth." Students can always use their notes, they can use their books, they can talk with each other, they can talk with me. Having taken hundreds of college units myself, from a science major to a design major, I learned that I was much more likely to *retain* the correct information if I *wrote down* the correct information. Rather than guessing and then writing down a wrong answer, the process of finding the correct answer on a test was much more productive. So I encourage you to bounce back and forth between the quiz and the answers, to discuss them with friends, and especially to apply the questions to other designed pages you see around you. "Open eyes" is the key to becoming more visually literate.

Listen to your eyes.

Answers: Quiz #1 (page 86)

Remove the border to open up space. New designers tend to put borders around everything. Stop it! Let it breathe! Don't contain it so tightly!

Proximity

The headings are too far away from their related items: *move them closer.*

There are double Returns above and below the headings: *take out all double Returns, but add a little extra space **above** the headings so they are more closely connected to the following material they belong with.*

Separate personal info from résumé items with a little extra space.

Alignment

Text is centered and flush left, and second lines of text return all the way to the left edge: create a strong flush left alignment—all heads align with each other, all bullets align, all text aligns, second lines of text align with first lines.

Repetition

There is already a repetition of the hyphen: *strengthen that repetition by making it a more interesting bullet and using it in front of every appropriate item.*

There is already a repetition in the headings: *strengthen that repetition by making the headings strong and black.*

The strong black impression in the bullets now repeats and reinforces the strong black in the headings.

Contrast

There isn't any: *use a strong, bold face for contrast of heads, including "Résumé" (to be consistent, or repetitive); add contrast with the strong bullets.*

By the way: the numbers in the new version use the "proportional oldstyle" form that is found in many OpenType fonts. If you don't have them, make the numbers a point size or two smaller so they don't call undue attention to themselves.

Answers: Quiz #2 (page 87)

Different typefaces: There are three different sans serifs, one serif face, one script, and one decorative. Choose two of those: perhaps the decorative face that's used in the title, plus a nice serif to imply classic grace.

Different alignments: Oh my gawd. Some elements are flush left, some are centered, some are centered in the middle of empty space, some have no connection or alignment with anything else in the world.

Strong line: The logo could provide a strong line against which to align other elements.

Lack of proximity: Group the information. You know what should be grouped together.

Lack of focal point: Several items are competing for attention. Choose one.

Lack of repetitive elements: The four logos do *not* qualify as repetitive elements—they are randomly placed in each corner merely to fill the empty corners; that is, they were not placed as conscious design elements. But perhaps you can pick up the color of the logo to use as a repetitive item.

Remove the boxes inside the border. Use square corners on the remaining border to reinforce the square corners of the logo and to keep the edges clean.

TAKE OFF THE CAPS LOCK!!!

The example on the next page is only one of many possibilities.

Draw lines along all the edges that now align.

The Shakespeare Papers

Shakespeare by Design

The Shakespeare Papers are bimonthly booklets of amusing, tantalizing, peculiar, educative, unexpected, brilliant, surprising, intriguing, and occasionally controversial tidbits about the Shakespearean plays and sonnets.

Subscription-based:
Only $38 a year for six collectible issues

7 Sweet Swan Lane
Cygnet City, CA 94536
505.424.7926
TheShakespearePapers.com
cleo@TheShakespearePapers.com

typefaces
Wade Sans Light
Brioso Pro Light
and Bold Italic

Answers: Quiz #3 (page 161)

Oldstyle:	As I remember, Adam
Modern:	High Society
Slab serif:	The enigma continues

Sans serif:	It's your attitude
Script:	Too Sassy for Words
Decorative:	At the Rodeo

Answers: Quiz #4
(page 162)

Giggle:	B
Jiggle:	C
Diggle:	A
Piggle:	A
Higgle:	C
Wiggle:	B

Answers: Quiz #5
(page 163)

Diggle:	C
Riggle:	A
Figgle:	B
Biggle:	D
Miggle:	D
Tiggle:	A

Answers: Quiz #6 (page 194)

Fancy Perfume: **Conflict.** There are too many similarities: they are both all caps; they are both about the same size; they are both "frufru" typefaces (kind of fancy); they are similar in weight.

Dogfood: **Contrast.** There is a strong contrast of size, color, form (both caps vs. lowercase and roman vs. italic), weight, and structure (although neither typeface has a definite thick/thin contrast in their strokes, the two faces are definitely built out of very different materials).

My Mother: **Conflict.** Although there is a contrast of form in the caps vs. lowercase, there are too many other similarities that conflict. The two faces are the same size, very similar weight, the same structure, and the same roman form. This is a twitcher.

Funny Farm: **Conflict.** There is potential here, but the differences need to be strengthened. There is a contrast of form in the caps vs. lower-case, and also in the extended face vs. the regular face. There is a slight contrast of structure in that one face has a gentle thick/thin transition and the other has monoweight, extended letters. Can you put your finger on the biggest problem? (Think a minute.) What is the focus here? "Health Insurance" is trying to be the focus by being larger, but it uses a light weight face. "Funny Farm" is trying to be the focus, even though it's smaller, by using all caps and bold. You have to decide which one is the boss and emphasize one of the concepts, either "Funny Farm" or "Health Insurance."

Let's Dance: **Contrast.** Even though they are exactly the same size and from the same family (the Formata family), the other contrasts are strong: weight, form (roman vs. italic and caps vs. lowercase), structure (from the weight contrasts), color (though both are black, the weight of "dance" gives it a darker color).

Answers: Quiz #7 (page 195)

1. **Don't.** Two scripts will conflict with each other because they usually have the same form.
2. **Don't.** Typefaces from the same category have the same structure.
3. **Don't.** They will fight with each other. Decide what is the most important and emphasize that item.
4. **Don't.** Most scripts and italics have the same form—slanted and flowing.
5. **Do.** You instantly have a strong contrast of structure and color.
6. **Do.** You instantly have a contrast of structure and color.
7. **Don't.** Two fancy faces will usually conflict because their fancy features both compete for attention.
8. **Don't.** Your purpose in putting type on a page is usually to communicate. Never forget that.
9. **Do.**
10. **Do.** The basic law of breaking the rules is to know what the rules are in the first place. If you can justify breaking the rules—and the result works—go ahead!

Typefaces in this Book

There are more than three hundred fonts, or typefaces, in this book. Now, when someone (especially a font vendor) tells you there are "a certain number" of fonts, they usually include all the variations of one font—the regular version is a font, the italic is another, the bold is another, etc. Since you are (or were) a new designer, I thought you might be interested in knowing exactly which fonts were used in this book. **Most fonts are shown in 14-point type,** unless otherwise noted. Have fun!

Primary faces

Main body text:	Warnock Pro Light, 10.5/14.25 (which means 10.5-point type with 14.25-point leading).
Chapter titles:	Bauer Bodoni Bold Condensed, 66/60
Chapter numbers:	Bauer Bodoni Roman, 225 point, 10 percent plum
Tiny little type:	Warnock Pro Caption (most of the time)
Main heads:	Silica Regular, 26/22
Captions:	Proxima Nova Alt Light, 9.5/11.5
Cover:	Glasgow

Modern

Bauer Bodoni Roman, *Italic*, **Bold Condensed**

Bodoni Poster, Poster Compressed

Didot Regular, **Bold**

Madrone

Mona Lisa Solid

Onyx Regular

(Berthold) Walbaum Book Regular, **Bold**

Times New Roman Bold

Oldstyle

Arno Pro Regular

New Baskerville Roman

Bernhard Modern

Brioso Pro Light, *Light Italic*,
Regular, *Regular Italic*,
Bold, ***Bold Italic***

Cochin Medium, *Italic*,
Bold, ***Bold Italic***

ITC Garamond Light,
Book, **Bold**, **Ultra**

Garamond Premier Pro
Regular, *Italic*

Golden Cockerel Roman

Goudy Oldstyle, *Italic*

Minister Light, *Light
Italic*, **Bold**

Palatino Light, *Italic*

Photina Regular, *Italic*

Times New Roman
Regular, *Italic*,
Bold, ***Bold Italic***

Adobe Jensen Pro Regular

Warnock Pro Light,
Light Italic, Regular,
Regular Italic, **Bold,
Bold Italic,**
Caption, Light Caption
(specifically for small type)

Slab serif

Aachen Bold

American Typewriter
Medium, **Bold**

Blackoak

**Clarendon Light,
Roman, Bold**

Memphis Light,
Medium, **Bold,
Extra Bold**

New Century
Schoolbook Roman

Silica Light, Extra Light,
Regular, **Bold, Black**

Sans serif

Antique Olive Roman, Black

Bailey Sans Book, **Bold, Extra Bold**

Cotoris Regular, *Italic,* Bold

Delta Jaeger Light, **Medium, Bold**

Eurostile Demi, Bold, Extended Two, Bold Extended Two, Bold Condensed

Folio Light, **Medium, Bold, Extra Bold**

Formata Light, **Regular, Medium, *Medium Italic,* Bold, *Bold Italic,* Bold Condensed,** Light Condensed

Franklin Gothic Book

Helvetica Regular, **Bold, *Bold Oblique***

Imago Extra Bold

Myriad Pro Condensed

Officina Sans Book, **Bold**

Optima Roman, *Oblique,* **Bold**

Proxima Nova Regular, **Black**

Proxima Nova Alt Light, **Semibold, Bold, Extra Bold**

Ronnia Regular, *Italic,* **Bold, *Bold Italic***

Shannon Book, *Book Oblique,* **Extra Bold**

Syntax Roman, **Bold, Black,**

Trade Gothic Light, Medium, *Medium Oblique,* Condensed No. 18, **Bold, Bold Condensed No. 20**

Trebuchet Regular, *Italic*

Universe 39 Thin Ultra Condensed, **65 Bold, 75 Black, 85 Extra Black**

Verdana Regular

Script

Anna Nicole

Arid

Bickham Script Pro
(24 point)

Carpenter (24 point)

Charme

Cocktail Shaker

Coquette Regular, **Bold**

Emily Austin (24 point)

Fountain Pen

Linoscript (20 point)

Milk Script

Ministry Script

Miss Fajardose (18 point)

Shelley Volante Script

Snell Roundhand Bold, Black

Spring Light, Regular

Tekton Regular, Oblique, **Bold**

Wendy Medium, Bold (24 point)

Viceroy

Ornaments

Birds

Diva Doodles

Gargoonies

MiniPics Lil Folks

MiniPics Head Buddies

Renfield's Lunch

Golden Cockerel Ornaments

Minion Pro (ornaments)

Type Embellishments One

Type Embellishments Two

Type Embellishments Three

Adobe Woodtype Ornaments 2

ITC Zapf Dingbats

Decorative

(all fonts below are 18 point)

Bodoni Classic
Bold Ornate

By George Titling

Canterbury Oldstyle

Blue Island

Coquette Regular,
Bold

Escaldio Gothico

FAJITA MILD

FLYSWIM

frances uncial

GLASGOW

Improv Regular

Industria Solid

Jiggery Pokery

JUNIPER

LITHOS
EXTRA LIGHT

PERCOLATOR EXPERT

Pious Henry

Potzrebie

SCARLETT

Schablone Rough

Schablone
Labelrough
Positive

Schmutz Cleaned

Scriptease

**Sneakers
Ultrawide**

Spumoni

Stoclet Light, **Bold**

Tabitha

Tapioca

THE WALL

Wade Sans Light

Zanzibar

Appendix

OpenType

When you set a typeface in a very large size, very small size, or average size for reading, the letterforms should be shaped a little differently for each size. Very small sizes need to be a wee bit heavier, and very large sizes need to be lighter or else the thin strokes become thick and clunky. But most typefaces on a computer use one standard matrix, say for size 12 point, and just enlarge or reduce it. Warnock Pro, however, is a collection of faces within the family that are specifically designed for the different uses of type. You can see below that the "Caption" font looks heavy at 20 point, but at 8 point it's perfect. The "Display" font looks a little scrawny at 8 point, but those thin strokes are just lovely when set larger. An OpenType Pro font also has the option to use these oldstyle lining figures (234987) or the tabular figures (234987), as well as several other options. If your computer and software are up-to-date, you can access up to 16,000 characters in one OpenType font, and you can use the same font file on both Macs and PCs.

Warnock Pro Caption
at 20 point

Warnock Pro Caption at 8 point

Warnock Pro Display
at 20 point

Warnock Pro Display at 8 point

Here is a Warnock Pro Regular W in gray directly behind the Display font W. You can clearly see the difference in the strokes.

Mini-glossary

The **baseline** is the invisible line on which type sits (see page 164).

Body copy, body text, or sometimes just plain **body** or **text** refers to the main block of text that you read, as opposed to headlines, subheads, titles, etc. Body text is usually set between 9- and 12-point type with 20 percent added between the lines.

A **bullet** is a little marker, typically used in a list instead of numbers, or between words. This is the standard bullet: •.

A **dingbat** is a small, ornamental character, like this: ■❖✔✍❤. You might have the fonts Zapf Dingbats or Wingdings, which are made up of dingbats.

Elements are the separate objects on the page. An element might be a single line of text, or a graphic, or a group of items that are so close together they are perceived as one unit. To know the number of elements on a page, squint your eyes and count the number of times your eye stops, as it notices each separate item.

Extended text refers to the body copy (as above) when there is a lot of it, as in a book or a long report.

Eye flow, or your **eye,** refers to your eyes as if they are an independent body. As a designer, you can control the way someone moves her "eye" around a page (the eye flow), so you need to become more conscious of how *your* eye moves around on the page. Listen to your eyes.

Justified type is when a block of text is lined up on both the left and right edges.

Resolution refers to how well an image appears to be "resolved"; that is, how clear and clean it looks to us. It's a complicated subject, but here is the gist:

Printed pages: Generally, images that will be printed on paper need to be 300 dpi (dots [of ink] per inch). Always check with the press that will print the job to find out what resolution they want. To get a 300 dpi image, use your image editing application (such as Photoshop) to resize the image *to the size it will be when printed*, and make it 300 ppi (pixels per inch).

For print, use **.tif** images, 300 dpi, CMYK color mode.

Screen pages: Images on the screen are 72 ppi (pixels per inch). These will look crummy when printed, but will look perfect on the screen. Use your image editing application (such as Photoshop) to resize the image *to the size it will appear on the screen.* This means if you have a thumbnail image linked to a larger image, you need *two* separate files of the same image!

For screen, use **.jpg** images, 72 ppi, RGB color mode.

A **rule** is a line, a drawn line, such as the one under the headline "Mini-glossary," above.

White space is the space on a page that is not occupied by any text or graphics. You might call it "blank" space. Beginners tend to be afraid of white space; professional designers use lots of white space.

Trapped white space is when the white, or blank, space on a page is trapped between elements (such as text or photos), with no space through which to flow.

Resources

Veer.com

MyFonts.com

iStockPhoto.com

Before & After Magazine; BAMagazine.com

Layers Magazine; LayersMagazine.com

InDesign PDF Magazine; InDesignMag.com

Index